STEM is Elementary:
Why Elementary Science, Technology, Engineering, and Mathematics Prepares Students to Beat the Gaps

Glory Oljace

STEM is Elementary, LLC
Bethel, Minnesota

Copyright © April 2012 by STEM is Elementary, LLC

PRINTING HISTORY
April 2012, STEM is Elementary, LLC
September 2012, STEM is Elementary, LLC
May 2013, STEM is Elementary, LLC
November 2013, STEM is Elementary, LLC

All rights reserved. No part of this book may be reproduced by any mechanical, photographic, or electronic process, or otherwise copied without permission in writing from STEM is Elementary, LLC. When forms and sample documents are included, their use is authorized only by educators, local school sites, and/or noncommercial or non-profit entities that have purchased the book.

Published by
STEM is Elementary, LLC
P.O. Box 26
Bethel, MN 55005

www.elementarystem.com

Table of Contents

Foreword to Expanded Edition[2]	5
Introduction	6
Why STEM Education?	9
Why *Elementary* STEM Education?	17
Standards and Assessments	22
Benefits of an Interdisciplinary Approach	28
Characteristics of Elementary STEM Classrooms	38
Writing the Yearlong Scope and Sequence	51
Writing the 10-Week Units	59
Designing Interdisciplinary STEM Lessons	82
Opportunities and Challenges	88
Summary: Why STEM is Elementary	93
Appendixes:	
References	95
STEM Resources	96
STEM Funding Sources	98
Books for Interdisciplinary Math Instruction	99
Books for Interdisciplinary Instruction	100

"Students learned science while incorporating, writing, music, art, movement and technology. What a great example of project-based-learning connected to standards!"
J. Doolittle, Media Specialist

"The lessons are outstanding and could be completed by a variety of grade levels."
B. Kulow, Southwest Iowa Regional STEM Manager

"I want to integrate subjects into my classroom with the same ease as you."
A. Hewitt, Student Teacher

"Thank you for bringing in the weather lady. I learned a lot about weather."
A. Brown, 8th Grade Student

"Your proposal was selected from a very competitive national pool of applications and demonstrates your extraordinary effort to bring excellence to your students."
H. Sanford, President and CEO of the NEA Foundation

"I'm elated to say that your book was a hit with our PD folks!"
H. Harris, Director NPRC, National Association of Elementary School Principals

"Glory has planned and lead school-wide events flawlessly."
C. Pierskalla, Math Specialist

"Glory gives with her whole heart. Loves her class. Yes, she's a great teacher.
Cameron and Bob, 2nd Grade Students

"I have observed Glory's considerable skills in working with staff, students and families."
J. Henke, Principal

"Glory has developed innovative teaching strategies, using grants she has written, to provide creative opportunities to teach standards-based curriculums."
L. Warfield, Elementary International Baccalaureate Programme Director

"Seeing all your students engaged, excited and so knowledgeable really made my day!"
J. Alfano, Minneapolis Public Schools Elementary STEM Director

"Glory's mind is open to what is best for the people, particularly the children in our school."
D. Malcolm, Family Liaison

"One cannot visit, observe or co-teach in Glory Oljace's classroom without leaving with a sense of excellence and professionalism occurring throughout."
G. Beyer, District Mentor

"Glory is a talented teacher. She is able to integrate science, math, technology, reading, journaling and cooperative group work into every lesson."
T. Edwards, Principal

"We are indebted to you for your expertise that you put into teaching everyday."
J. Wampler, Parent of Student

"I was at the E4 conference where I attended your workshop. I thought you were amazing and I want to be in your classroom!"
C. Goding, Elementary Education

Foreword to the Expanded Edition[2]

I'm pleased and proud to say that I'm wrapping up my 23rd year of teaching. I graduated summa cum laude from Eastern Michigan University in 1990 with a major in elementary education and minors in science and mathematics. The majority of my career has been pleasantly spent at Pillsbury Elementary School in northeast Minneapolis as a classroom teacher. I've shared with over 600 children the thrill of science and the rewards of learning.

My love for science, technology, engineering, and mathematics has always been at the core of my instruction for one simple reason, STEM to an elementary-age student is magic. When children study STEM, they are learning so much more than just science, technology, engineering, and mathematics. They are really learning to communicate through writing, reading, speaking, and listening as well as critical thinking, and teamwork activities. Each of these disciplines is necessary for any STEM experience.

Surprisingly, the process I've developed for creating and implementing standards-based, interdisciplinary STEM-focused instruction is simple to do.

Glory Oljace
glory@elementarystem.com

Introduction

STEM captures the interest that leads to achievement.

Glory Oljace, 2012

In 1991, my husband and I moved to Minnesota for my dream job of teaching in a third and fourth grade multi-age classroom at Pillsbury Math Science Technology Elementary School in Minneapolis. I loved it! My colleagues and I inspired children, many of who went on to careers in STEM (science, technology, engineering, and mathematics) fields. The Pillsbury staff worked collaboratively with the support of the district, state, and national governments in preparing students to lead the future. Unfortunately as the economy, population growth, and feelings towards education changed, so did Pillsbury MST. Teachers with math, science or technology backgrounds began to leave the school when literacy instruction became the new focal point for all elementary instruction. And although outstanding teachers came in to replace exiting STEM teachers, the MST at Pillsbury was no more.

Sadly, these changes were not unique to Pillsbury. As the century changed, so did the public's thoughts on education. There was a national outcry for educational reforms. Studies began revealing that U.S. students were not achieving at acceptable levels. The fact that there was not a common agreement as to what acceptable levels were compounded the issue. Under the Bush Administration of 2002, the No Child Left Behind Act was enacted and districts across the country started to reform. Teachers began using *better* grade specific objectives (later to be called standards) focusing on reading and math primarily. Scores from newly developed tests would now be the measures as to whether students were achieving (adequate), and if schools were in need of improvement (failing.) Science, technology and engineering, along with social studies, project-based learning, music, art, physical education, and recess, were now considered to be the "extras," or the unnecessary parts to a child's elementary education. New tests meant the development and implementation of new reading, writing, and mathematics curriculums. Districts quickly adopted these new curriculums in hopes of preparing students for the mandated, high-stakes tests.

The President's Council of Advisors on Science and Technology summarized the troubling effects that the No Child Left Behind Act has had on student learning and quality STEM teachers:

> "Schools often lack teachers who know how to teach science and mathematics effectively – and who know and love their subject well enough to inspire their students. Teachers lack adequate support, including appropriate professional development as well as interesting and intriguing curricula. As a result, too many American students conclude early in their education that STEM subjects are boring, too difficult, or unwelcoming, leaving them ill-prepared to meet the challenges that will face their generation, their country, and the world."
>
> (PCAST, 2010)

Although the entire force of the change was well intended – to develop more rigorous schooling for students – educators did what they often do. They *threw out the baby with the bath water.* It was unnecessary and unacceptable to rid students' education of what was now considered "the extras" in order to teach reading and math exclusively. Several studies indicate that U.S. students lag behind other countries in critical thinking, socialization, and creativity. It's not surprising that they are also below average in science and math, and only slightly above average in reading. (OECD, 2012) "At a time when the need for more STEM education is critical, many STEM teams or programs are being eliminated or reduced." (PCAST, 2010) The United States needs to recognize that elementary level STEM programs are a viable solution to closing the achievement and opportunity gaps that exist within our country.

Over the years, using my love for science and math as the foundation, I have developed and refined a process for designing STEM-focused instruction that motivates learners, is standards-based, and provides all students with the needed tools to lead the future. The process, besides being rigorous and engaging for learners, also makes teachers' jobs easier. The method is based upon the Common Core State Standards in English language arts and mathematics, the Next Generation Science Standards as well as individual states' standards in science, social studies, technology, and the arts. The establishment of common standards is a huge bonus for educators. The Common Core State Standards and the Next Generation Science Standards were developed by educators from across the country to ensure that all students achieve, regardless of location. They are well written, easy to follow and developmentally appropriate – I like them. The STEM instructional design process that I have developed always begins with the standards. Every lesson and experience is tied to a measurable benchmark that integrates learning to mirror real life and makes it relevant to students. Due to its interdisciplinary structure, the model also relieves elementary teachers of planning and preparing for up to seven different curriculums daily. There is finally enough time in the day to teach all subjects and to do justice to each one. Interdisciplinary STEM programming motivates learners and teachers alike.

Chapter 1

Why STEM Education?

The Nation's future depends on our ability to educate today's students in science, technology, engineering, and mathematics – STEM.

President's Council of Advisors on Science and Technology, 2010

In the past decade a new acronym, in the already acronym packed field of education, has taken center stage – STEM. Science, Technology, Engineering, and Mathematics. Although the term seems to be popping up everywhere it is not easily understood. Judith Ramaley is credited with the naming of STEM in 2001. She was the director of the National Science Foundation's education and human resources division at the time. Ms. Ramaley and her colleagues were working to develop curriculum that would enhance education in science, mathematics, engineering, and technology. During her work and discussions, the term SMET was used to label the research. Ramaley said, "I didn't like the sound of that word," and offered STEM as an alternative. She believed science and mathematics were the natural bookends for technology and engineering. Not only did STEM capture the relationship amongst disciplines, it sounded better than SMET. Regardless, Ramaley's term was coined and STEM was launched. (Christenson, 2011)

STEM has grown in the years since its naming. Yet planning, implementing, and assessing STEM education can be difficult. The most commonly accepted definition of STEM education used by educators is:

> "STEM is an interdisciplinary approach to learning where rigorous academic concepts are coupled with real-world lessons as students apply science, technology, engineering, and mathematics in contexts that make connections between school, community, work, and the global enterprise enabling the development of STEM literacy and with it the ability to compete in the new economy."
>
> (Tsupros, Kohler, and J. Hallinen, 2009)

It is easy to understand why people are confused about what STEM really means. Basically, STEM education is an interdisciplinary approach towards learning that uses science, technology, engineering, and mathematics to engage learners and prepares them to compete effectively in the 21st century.

Science is at the base of STEM for many reasons. The most obvious is that science engages all learners. Science taps in to students' natural curiosity, and provides a structure and relevance for learning. Quality science instruction connects and enhances understanding in mathematics, writing, reading, speaking, listening, critical thinking, teamwork, and community building. And, it is particularly important to our underrepresented students. (NSF, 2013) A key finding from 15 years of public opinion surveys, conducted by the Bayer Corporation, was "Science literacy is critical for Americans young and old, scientist or non-scientist." (Bayer, 2012) This is a powerful and exciting statement. Science is a natural springboard for learning across disciplines. It allows for project-based, student-centered environments, and is most of all motivating.

The effective use of technology is critical to students' success in an ever-changing global economy. Technology not only assists with the efficient communication of knowledge, it can also make teachers' jobs easier. Yet, technology does not focus entirely on electronics or digital sources. In fact, the serious use of the term only dates back about 50 years. (Satell, 2013) More accurately, technology is the use of tools to make tasks easier and to help solve problems. It is the process by which humans modify nature to meet their needs and wants.

Engineering is the part of STEM that is probably the least understood. In the real world, science and engineering are not neatly divided. Simply defined, scientists answer questions about the world around them, while engineers modify the world based upon humans' wants and needs. Yet, science and engineering are intricately connected because engineers apply science and mathematical concepts, using technology, to design solutions to complex issues. In the classroom, engineering is seen when students work in groups or independently to find answers to a variety of situations. Students in high school may design and construct an energy efficient house, while elementary students might design and build a model of a house for a stuffed animal. Regardless of the task, successful STEM programs have students applying science, mathematics, and technology in the creation of practical solutions. This is engineering.

Mathematics is the most recognized and understood aspect of STEM. It is also the one discipline, due to its somewhat linear progression, that cannot always be integrated into STEM instruction. This makes sense to most people. For example, elementary students must be able to recognize the number five, and understand what five means before using five in more abstract situations. Similarly, middle school students must have a deep understanding of rational numbers before solving complex algebraic equations. But, even though math is taught in isolation during certain phases of a student's STEM education, this does not mean that math is not interdisciplinary. STEM students are critical and flexible thinkers who apply their mathematical understandings in solving complex real-world problems. They are mathematicians.

So why is interdisciplinary STEM education needed in the United States? The main reason is that STEM-focused programming can positively impact our national economy. STEM employment makes up only a small fraction of the U.S. employment total, yet it has grown quickly. According to data collected by the Bureau of Labor Statistics employment in STEM fields grew considerably between the years 1993 and 2007. The Bureau of Labor Statistics also predicts increased growth in STEM job openings through 2014. (Solis & Hall, 2011) "In 2010, there were 7.6 million STEM workers in the United States, representing about 1 in 18 workers." (Landgon, McKittrick, Beede, Khan & Doms, 2011) The U.S.

Department of Commerce Economics and Statistics Administration similarly reports STEM occupations growing three times as fast as non-STEM occupations. The department also projects STEM jobs to grow by 17.0 percent from 2008 to 2018, compared to a 9.8 percent growth for non-STEM occupations.

Higher than average earnings often indicates a strong demand for workers. STEM workers earned on average 26 percent more than the national average in 2005. (Fudge, 2013) A Bureau of Labor Statistics report from May 2011 states STEM occupations to be high paying. The report also lists the mean wage for all STEM occupations as $77,880 in May 2009, while the mean wage for all non-STEM occupations was $43,460. (Cover, Jones & Watson, 2011) In addition to high job growth and higher earnings, workers in STEM fields on average experience lower unemployment rates than workers in other fields. The unemployment rate for STEM workers rose from 1.8 percent in 2007 to 5.3 percent in 2010, while the unemployment rate for non-STEM workers rose from 4.8 percent for non-STEM workers to almost 10 percent for the same time period. (Landgon, McKittrick, Beede, Khan & Doms, 2011) Job opening in STEM occupations outnumbers unemployed workers by 2 to 1 according to U.S. Representative Marcia Fudge.

This is great news for post-secondary STEM graduates and workers, but not for the remaining work-age population. The United States has a serious problem. We cannot fill the need for STEM workers because the United States continues to fall further behind other countries in preparing and inspiring our students to lead in STEM fields. (PCAST, 2010) While the number of U.S. degrees awarded in STEM fields has risen slightly over the past five years, only 15.6 percent of bachelor's degrees awarded were in STEM fields. This compares to 46.7 percent of STEM degrees awarded in China. (NSB, 2010) What is even more troubling is the loss of interest in STEM disciplines amongst U.S. students. Nearly 28 percent of high school freshman express an interest in STEM-related fields – about 100,000 students every year. Unfortunately, of these learners, more than 57 percent lose interest in STEM before graduation. The research clearly indicates a lack of interest or preparation in STEM fields amongst U.S. students.

The President's Council of Advisors on Science and Technology in a Report to the President noted that in addition to academic and interest gaps in the United States in STEM, there is a large opportunity gap as well. Due to these gaps:

> "African Americans, Hispanics, Native Americans, and women are seriously underrepresented in many STEM fields, which limits their participation in many well-paid, high-growth professions."
> (PCAST, 2010)

The National Science Foundation recently shared a statistical analysis entitled *Women, Minorities, and Persons with Disabilities in Science and Engineering: 2013*. The study found that the science and engineering workforce is mostly white and male, and is not representative of the nation's workforce as a whole. In fact, the participation of women and minorities in science and engineering is much lower. Minority women make up only 1 in 10 of employed scientists and engineers. (NSF, 2013) The lack of female STEM workers was also highlighted in a 2012 report from the Institute for Women's Policy Research as well. The analysis revealed a 6.3 percent decline in women earning associate degrees or certificates in STEM fields from 1997 to 2007.

STEM workers not only fuel our economy with higher incomes and spending, they also produce innovation and entrepreneurship. Unfortunately, the United States has lost its innovative and competitive edge in the last 10 years as reported by the Information Technology and Innovation Foundation, a research and educational think tank. A July 2011 *Information Technology and Innovation Foundation's Atlantic Century II* report ranked the United States sixth out of 40 industrialized nations in innovative competiveness. (Atkinson & Andes, 2011) In January 2010, the Milken Institute, an economic think tank, ranked the United States eighth out of 110 countries. (DeVol & Wong, 2010) Yet the Information Technology and Innovation Foundation's report also looked at the rate of change in innovative capacity. The United States ranked last out of 40 countries!

> "The supply of [U.S.] STEM workers is not meeting businesses' needs. And this is jeopardizing our nation's ability to drive innovation and competiveness and seize a global advantage."
> (Schiavelli, 2011)

The educational performance gap between the United States and other countries also continues to grow according to the Organization for Economic Cooperation and Development, an assembly of 65 countries founded to stimulate economic progress and world trade. Every three years the organization conducts assessments in reading, science and mathematics for industrialized countries. The examinations called the Program for International Student Assessment are international benchmarks for evaluating the reading, science and mathematical literacy of 15-year-old students. The 2006 and 2009 scores show the United States ranked 25th in math and 24th in science out of 30 industrialized countries. (OECD, 2007) In 2009, the Organization for Economic Cooperation and Development added reading to the assessment scores rankings. And, guess what? After spending millions of dollars to improve our nation's reading scores, due to the No Child Left Behind Act, and to the detriment of other disciplines, the United States still did not shine compared to other countries. Even though our reading score ranking was 21 out of 40 countries, the score was just 7 points above the world average. This is nothing to celebrate.

The results also revealed a troubling trend for U.S. female students. In a representative sample of 15-year-olds from around the world, girls generally outperform boys in science. This is true for every country except the United States. Why is that? Andreas Schleicher, who oversees the tests, explains that different countries offer different incentives for pursuing math and science. In the United States, boys "see science as something that effects their life." And, there is also the "stereotype threat." Schleicher says that early in childhood, from about age 4, gender roles in occupations appear to be formed. (Fairfield and McLean, 2012) Experts say these gender influences are strong in the United States, Britain and Canada, but are less persistent in Russia, Asia and the Middle East. In Jordan, girls' consistently scored more than 8 percent higher than the boys' on the science portion of the Program for International Student Assessment tests. According to the Commission on Professionals in Science and Technology women compromised nearly half of all U.S. paid workers in 2000, yet they held just one quarter of U.S. STEM jobs. (Pantic, 2007) The evidence suggests the critical need to engage our country's females in STEM education, and overcome the biases towards acceptable professions for women.

The following charts show the United States' PISA (Program for International Student Assessment) rankings in comparison to other countries for mathematics, science, and reading. Take note of the countries that ranked higher and lower than the United States. There are some surprises.

PISA Scores

Mathematics

Finland	548
Korea	547
Netherlands	531
Switzerland	530
Canada	527
Japan	523
New Zealand	522
Belgium	520
Austria	520
Denmark	513
Czech Republic	510
Iceland	506
Austria	505
Germany	504
Sweden	502
Iceland	501
France	496
United Kingdom	495
Poland	495
Slovak Republic	492
Hungary	491
Luxembourg	490
Norway	490
Spain	480
UNITED STATES	**474**
Portugal	466
Italy	462
Greece	459
Turkey	424
Mexico	406

Science

Korea	552
Finland	548
Canada	527
New Zealand	522
Netherlands	519
Australia	516
Switzerland	514
Belgium	511
Japan	511
Ireland	509
Sweden	505
Denmark	504
Poland	502
Germany	499
Austria	498
Czech Republic	496
United Kingdom	495
Iceland	495
France	492
Norway	487
Hungary	487
Luxembourg	485
Slovak Republic	479
UNITED STATES	**474**
Spain	470
Portugal	469
Italy	465
Greece	459
Turkey	436
Mexico	408

Reading

Shanghai-China	556
Korea	539
Finland	536
Hong Kong-China	549
Singapore	526
Canada	524
New Zealand	521
Japan	520
Australia	515
Netherlands	508
Belgium	506
Norway	503
Estonia	503
Switzerland	501
Iceland	500
Poland	500
UNITED STATES	**500**
Liechtenstein	499
Sweden	497
Germany	497
Ireland	496
Chinese Taipei	495
France	496
Denmark	495
United Kingdom	494
Hungary	494
Portugal	489
Macao-China	487
Italy	486
Latvia	484

Source: OECD

Research from a variety of world-recognized organizations strongly supports the need for STEM education at all levels. In order to capture the interests of future innovators, we must provide meaningful STEM-focused experiences today. The President's Council of Advisors on Science and Technology in a September 2010 Report to the President concluded:

> "To meet our needs for a STEM-capable citizenry, a STEM-proficient workforce, and future STEM experts, the Nation must focus on two complementary goals: We must prepare all students, including girls and minorities who are underrepresented in these fields, to be proficient in STEM subjects. And we must inspire all students to learn STEM and, in the process, motivate many of them to pursue STEM careers."
>
> (PCAST, 2010)

Chapter 2

Why Elementary STEM Education?

Grade-school children do not think as simplistically about STEM subjects as conventional curricula assume. They are capable of grasping both concrete examples and abstract concepts at remarkably early ages.

President's Council of Advisors on Science and Technology, 2010

I cannot remember any specific science instruction I received as a child until 9th Grade Physical Science. I am sad to admit I did horribly in the class. It was all about keeping track of an experiment and making conclusions based upon the data collected. What? This was my first experience at being asked to do this, and honestly, I had no idea or interest in continuing with learning science. However, since it was required, I continued through 11th Grade Chemistry. My feelings about science did not change in the following years. At the end of my sophomore year of college, when I was required to take any science course in order to become a junior, I took Physical Geology 101. It was a life changing experience. The teacher's expertise in delivering his love for science inspired me. I ended up minoring in science and mathematics and have inspired over 600 elementary scientists and mathematicians, many who have gone on into STEM fields. I know that beginning STEM-based learning in elementary school works.

Unfortunately, if you have been teaching in any elementary school, anywhere in the United States, you know that the current educational reforms do not support what educators know about elementary-age students. A large body of research conducted over the past decades has demonstrated how children learn math, science, engineering, and technology. Students who are immersed in multisensory experiences have shown increased motivation and achievement. (PCAST, 2010) Early exposure to STEM programs is especially important for minority and female students, who are underrepresented in STEM fields. In April of 2012, the Bayer Corporation published their analysis of 15 years of *Bayer Facts of Science Education Surveys.* The surveys polled diverse audiences on their attitudes towards science and technology, science education, science literacy, and STEM. The publication identified 15 universal beliefs that were common amongst all stakeholders. The findings most significant to elementary students are:

- Improving science education for all students – especially girls and underrepresented minorities should be a national priority and begin at the earliest possible elementary school level since that is where the STEM workforce truly begins.
- Science interest and ability are color-blind and gender-neutral: from an early age, boys and girls of all races and ethnic backgrounds are interested in science.
- In elementary school, science should be the "4th R" and given the same emphasis as reading, writing and mathematics.
- A hands-on, minds-on approach to science education is the best way for students to learn science and build crucial science literacy skills, such as critical thinking, problem solving and the ability to work in teams.

(Bayer, 2012)

These are just a few of the reasons why it is so important to capture students' STEM interest early. The National Research Council further supports the need for STEM programming at the elementary level. Their research verifies the effectiveness of "active learning," which occurs when students are fully engaged in building relationships, making connections between teachers, classmates and the environment. (NRC, 2011) Key conclusions from another National Research Council study were:

> "Students learn science by actively engaging in the practices of science, including conducting investigations; sharing ideas with peers; specialized ways of talking and writing; mechanical, mathematical, and computer-based modeling; and development of representations of phenomena."
> (NRC, 2007)

We could easily insert the word STEM in place of science, and the conclusions would still hold true.

Remember when at one time, kindergarten was a time for socializing, playing at the sand table, going to the play kitchen, or using your creativity at the dress-up area. Students were learning how to be learners. Sadly, today's kindergarten classrooms show little resemblance. Students in kindergarten are now expected to be reading and writing by mid-year. There is no time for "play," and certainly no time for STEM. A different report by the National Research Council further supports the importance social interaction has on learning:

> "A classroom environment that provides opportunities for students to participate in scientific practices includes scientific tasks embedded in social interaction using the discourse of science and work with scientific representations and tools. Each of these aspects requires support for student learning of scientific practices."
>
> (NRC, 2007)

Students need time to "play," interact with others and the environment, and learn how to be learners.

These unfortunate changes in education continue throughout the grades. Year by year subjects, projects, units, and "the extras" disappear. At first, it's barely noticed. Until one year, all that is left is reading, writing and mathematics. That's it: reading, writing and math. With all of that sacrifice, we thankfully have good readers and mathematicians. Right? Regrettably, we do not. The United States has slightly above average readers, and significantly below average mathematicians according to the Program for International Student Assessment scores rankings. The critical thinkers, who are able to work cooperatively and productively, are slowly disappearing. Since scores from federally mandated assessments now determine schools' success or failure, portions of all U.S. students' days are spent on uninspiring test preparation.

Why is that? We have lost sight of the fact that the skills students learn through STEM-based K–12 programs are enormous and have implications far into the future. Best practices for STEM are similar to best practices for education in general. This should not be surprising, but as stated in a 2011 National Research Council report, "It is important to pay attention to these [best] practices in STEM because the research suggests that some strategies are unique to STEM learning and some challenges particularly affect success in STEM." Other studies, according U.S. Representative Marcia Fudge, show that students exposed to STEM educational resources at young ages perform better in science and math than students who are not.

The No Child Left Behind Act has also changed the time spent on STEM instruction according to the Center on Education Policy. As part of an ongoing study of the impact of the No Child Left Behind Act, the organization conducted a deeper analysis of 2006 - 2007 survey data on the amount of instructional time devoted to specific subjects. The analysis showed that at the elementary grades, the main instructional focus was on mathematics and English language arts because those subjects are tested annually under current accountability systems. Listed below are key findings from the study:

- The shifts in instructional time toward English language arts (ELA) and mathematics and away from other subjects were relatively large in a majority of school districts. Districts that increased instructional time for ELA and/or math did so by 43%, on average. Districts that also reduced instructional time in other subjects reported average reductions of 32%.
- Eight out of ten districts that reported increasing time for English language arts did so by at least 75 minutes per week, and more than half (54%) did so by 150 minutes or more per week. Among districts that reported adding time for math, 63% added at least 75 minutes per week, and 19% added 150 minutes or more per week.
- Most districts that increased time for ELA or math also reported substantial cuts in time for other subjects or periods, including social studies, science, art and music, physical education, recess, or lunch.
- Among the districts that reported both increasing time for ELA or math and reducing time in other subjects, 72% indicated that they reduced time by a total of at least 75 minutes per week for one or more of these other subjects.

(McMurrer, 2008)

Even though there has been significant attention given to STEM education in the past few years, most of it has been directed at the high school and post-secondary levels. We are forgetting the nation's youngest learners. Elementary level STEM programs are critical to our future success in innovation and technology. Students cannot be expected to think critically for the first time in STEM subjects in middle school or beyond if they have not had the opportunity to experience STEM throughout the elementary grades. If you were to ask any adult what they remember from elementary school, I can assure you that they will not say, "I loved pages 152-189 from the blue reader," but rather they will remember a project where they were immersed in a study crossing many disciplines.

In 2010, the International Journal of Science Education published a paper that examined the events reported by scientists and graduate students regarding the experiences that first engaged them in science. The majority of the participants, 65 percent, stated that their interest in science began before middle school. (Maltese & Tai, 2010) The President's Council of Advisors on Science and Technology also reported that, "Boys and girls who show interest in STEM in eighth grade can be three times more likely to pursue degrees in STEM fields." What this suggests is the importance of providing STEM experiences during the elementary years.

The Obama administration has recommended the creation of 1,000 new highly-STEM-focused schools. The best part is that of the new STEM schools, 800 are designated for the elementary and middle school levels. STEM-based instruction can begin right in kindergarten. The report further states:

> "Studies suggest that achieving expertise is less a matter of innate talent than of having the opportunity and motivation to dedicate oneself to the study of a subject in a productive, intellectual way – and for sufficient time – to enable the brain development needed to think like a scientist, mathematician, or engineer."

I see proof of this every day. In fact, my current second grade students are some of the best scientists, mathematicians, and engineers I know. The report concludes:

> "Conventional approaches to teaching science and math have sometimes been shaped by misconceptions about what children cannot learn rather than focusing on students' innate curiosity, reasoning skills, and intimate observations of the natural world.."
>
> (PCAST, 2010)

Thankfully, leaders from diverse fields are beginning to support what educators have known for years. Elementary STEM programs work.

Chapter 3

Standards and Assessments

To be broadly prepared to participate and compete in a world economy driven by STEM-based innovations, our students need a common, strong foundation of knowledge and skills.

President's Council of Advisors on Science and Technology, 2010

The use of shared educational standards is not a new concept. Standards-based education reform has been a topic of discussion for decades. Under the Clinton administration, a standards-based vision was enacted in federal law with the 1994 reauthorization of the Elementary and Secondary Education Act and continued under the Bush administration with the No Child Left Behind Act of 2001. (P.L. 107, 2002) Unfortunately, what resulted from the Act was a decline in student achievement and teacher effectiveness. Yet, a positive result of the discord was the creation and implementation of rigorous common standards and assessments. (Carmichael, Martino, Porter-Magee & Wilson, 2010) Education stakeholders from across the country have worked collaboratively to establish rigorous shared standards and assessments. They are internationally benchmarked to provide every student, regardless of location, a world-class education, as well as prepare teachers in the design and implementation of quality instruction.

Common Core State Standards

The Common Core State Standards Initiative is a state-led effort coordinated by the National Governors Association Center for Best Practices and the Council of Chief State School Officers. According to their website, the standards were developed by teachers, parents, school administrators, and experts from across the United States to ensure that all students acquire the needed skills to lead the future. They are benchmarked to international standards to guarantee that U.S. students are competitive in the emerging global economy. ("Frequently asked questions," 2012) They are well written, easy to follow, developmentally appropriate, and necessary. I like them.

The Fordham Institute, an educational policy think tank, analyzed the English language arts and mathematics standards in 2010 using a 10-point grading system measuring content, rigor, clarity, and specificity. The final report issued found that the Common Core State Standards were clearly superior to those in use at the time in thirty-nine states in math and thirty-seven states in English. In thirty-nine states, the Common Core State Standards were superior in both math and reading. (Byrd-Carmichael, Martino, Porter-Magee & Wilson, 2010) As of May of 2013, all but five states have formally adopted the Common Core State Standards in English language arts and mathematics. Of the non-adopting states, Minnesota, Nebraska, and Alaska, had state standards that were in the "clearly inferior" to the Common Core State Standards category.* The other two states, Texas and Virginia, had standards that were in the "too close to call" category, meaning that they are at least as clear and rigorous as the Common Core State Standards. All but one of the adopting states reported having developed some type of formal implementation plan for transitioning to the new shared standards, with Wyoming indicating work on its plan is underway. (Porter, Riley, Towne, Hightower, Lloyd, Sellers & Swanson, 2012) As an elementary educator, I am encouraged by the fact that states have united to bring our students a rigorous, high-quality education.

---

* In defense of my home state of Minnesota, the Department of Education cannot amend, repeal, nor adopt any academic standards and assessments without legislative authorization. This means that Minnesota is required by law to keep the current academic standards and assessments in place until otherwise constituted. (Larson, 2006)

A further indicator of the United States commitment to common standards is the unveiling of the Next Generation Science Standards. They are interdisciplinary by design, require students to solve real-world problems, and prepare educators to better serve the needs of all students.

Next Generation Science Standards

The Next Generation Science Standards were written by diverse groups of science stakeholders from 26 states. According to its website, the standards "are rich in content and practice and are arranged in a coherent manner across disciplines and grades to ensure all students an internationally benchmarked science education." ("Developing next generation science standards," 2013) They differ from previous versions in several ways. Most appreciated is that they recognize teacher expertise and student individuality. Every standard is clearly defined with performance expectations. Each performance expectation is a statement as to what students should be able to do after instruction. They are not a list of required tasks or assessments. Instead, performance expectations outline various approaches for evaluating student achievement.

Specific lessons are not required or even needed, because mastery can be demonstrated in countless ways. The following third grade Next Generation Science Standard could be assessed differently to meet the unique needs of students and staff.

> 3.PS2-1: Plan and conduct an investigation to provide evidence of the effects of balanced and unbalanced forces on the motion of an object.

For example, a third grade classroom might use their understanding from various experiences with Newton's of Motion to present a Bill Nye-like presentation to show mastery of the standard. While another third grade classroom might design a miniature golf course for students to play, and exhibit the science concepts involved.

The integrated structure of the Next Generation Science Standards also provides opportunities for student learning across disciplines. They were written to include logical connections with the Common Core State Standards in English language arts and mathematics, and crosscutting concepts in technology and engineering. Yet, what I appreciate most as a classroom teacher is that the Next Generation Science Standards recognize my expertise in creating and implementing rigorous instruction. They are not based on any particular curriculum or combination of curriculums. Instead, the Next Generation Science Standards are founded on a set of international benchmarks that ensures every student a world-class education and prepares them for success in the 21st century.

Common standards could provide a focus for teacher preparation programs as well. Having mentored a number of practicum students over the years, I have noticed that even the best-trained teacher candidates often lack confidence or knowledge of basic scientific concepts. This is the result of K-12 education and teacher preparation programs' forced focus on reading and mathematics. Yet, by understanding the positive impact STEM education has on student success, and with the support of the Next Generation Science Standards, colleges can direct changes in educational best practices. Studies have shown that there is a significant effect on students' test scores and learning when prospective educators are prepared to teach the curriculum that they will be using. (Boyd, Grossman, Lankford, Loeb & Wyckoff, 2009) It simply would not matter which university a teacher graduates from if all states shared the same standards. Every graduate, regardless of location, would be prepared in teaching standards-based lessons founded on world-class benchmarks developed by experts nationwide. Teacher preparation programs would have the advantage of designing more specific courses to address the needs of the next generation of learners, and could help guide the creation of instructional materials, textbooks, and assessments based on common standards.

Collaboration amongst states' educators and experts is perhaps the most beneficial aspect of common standards movement. Shared standards could provide the perfect format for establishing STEM networks to support the collaboration between educators and experts nationwide. As a result of this collaboration, the United States could lead in the creation of consistent high academic standards that improve our ability to serve the needs of students and prepares them to compete in the global economy.

Common Assessments

Shared standards are only a component in creating world-class educational programming for all students. Common assessments are also needed to ensure all students have the skills needed to achieve in the 21st century. Unfortunately, the current evaluations do not provide the data needed to ensure all students' success. Most educators are frustrated with the number and quality of current mandated assessments. Even though, all stakeholders recognize the importance of standards and assessments, the problem is deciding on which ones to use. "Standards should be aimed not at memorizing facts but at achieving a combination of factual knowledge, conceptual understanding, procedural skills, and habits of thought. Assessments should measure the extent to which students have mastered this full range of learning." (PCAST, 2010) The majority of schools in the United States require by law state summative assessments. Sadly, these high-stakes tests cannot accurately measure student success. They only offer a quick snapshot of students' understanding on a particular day. The results of these evaluations often show U.S. students lagging behind other countries in science, mathematics, and literacy. Yet, in hopes of scoring higher on the assessments, districts make the mistake of devoting precious instructional time to test prep. This has resulted in a generation of learners who are unable to think critically or work cooperatively.

The goal of assessment is to evaluate student learning. Summative assessments usually occur at the end of an instructional unit, while formative assessments are continually used throughout to monitor student achievement. In a world economy that is becoming increasingly less content and skill specific, U.S. students need to be able to apply knowledge in a variety of contexts to solve complex issues. Shared summative assessments that measure what students need to know, and that are aligned with the standards are needed. Although it may at first seem cost and time prohibitive, the collaboration between states in the design and implementation of shared assessments could actually provide huge savings. Assessments aligned to internationally benchmarked standards could provide more specific and accurate student achievement data as well. Educational publishers would be inclined to develop curricular materials to match what educators and students require – reliable and relevant assessments. Common assessments would help students and teachers alike.

Most STEM educators plan instruction based upon data collected through ongoing formative assessments. They become experts in quickly gauging students' understanding of important concepts. They can assess, change course, and reteach all within the same lesson. Elementary STEM educators recognize that exit slips or a thumb up or down can provide as much information as weekly tests or quizzes, and are easier to adminster. The environment is child-centered and project-based. As a result, students' understanding is often evaluated though writing, presentations, projects, self-assessments, or peer-assessment. STEM students take responsibility for measuring their own achievement, and are often involved in the development of authentic assessments.

Interdisciplinary STEM education provides the ideal structure for delivering rigorous standards-based programming. Leaders across the nation are beginning to realize the impact STEM has on student success. Legislation recently introduced by Senator Al Franken of Minnesota and Senator Jeff Merkley of Oregon will help to improve student achievement in STEM fields and subjects through shared standards and assessments. Senator Franken said, "Our nation's future competitiveness in the global economy depends on how well we prepare our students in STEM fields, and right now we're lagging behind." The President's Council of Advisors on Science and Technology summarizes the need for shared standards succinctly:

> "Shared standards create the need and opportunity to provide better materials and professional development for teachers and to lay the groundwork for fair and valid assessments that measure what students have learned and benchmark U.S. performance against that of other countries."
> (PCAST, 2010)

Thankfully, all education stakeholders are feeling the urgency in creating elementary STEM-focused programs that are standards-based to support students and teachers alike.

Chapter 4

Benefits of an Interdisciplinary Approach

STEM-focused elementary schools could also provide a unique opportunity to better connect science learning and literacy. Currently, reading and science are generally taught as distinct subject areas, and the potential for synergies between the two areas of learning are often overlooked.

President's Council of Advisors on Science and Technology, 2010

In today's world where the communication of knowledge and information happens every second of the day, individuals who are fluent in several disciplines, and who can easily move between them will prosper. Interdisciplinary instruction fosters creativity, adaptability, critical reasoning, and collaboration. (Jacobs, 1989) An integrated approach towards learning is effective because it not only allows students to develop expertise in many disciplines, and helps them to grasp the important role interrelationships play in the real world.

Interdisciplinary education is an instructional method that integrates subjects in a comprehensive manner, enabling students to develop meaningful understandings, and the ability to view connections between disciplines on selected topics. Studies have repeatedly shown the positive impact interdisciplinary learning has on student achievement and teacher effectiveness. One of the conclusions, from a National Research

Council report on how children learn science and math, stated:

> "Many existing national, state, and local standards and assessments, as well as the typical curricula in use in the United States, contain too many disconnected topics given equal priority. Too little attention is given to how students' understanding of a topic can be supported and enhanced. As a result, topics receive repeated, shallow coverage with little consistency, which provides a fragile foundation for further knowledge growth."
>
> (NRC, 2007)

Interdisciplinary instruction works for two main reasons. One, it's motivating for students and can lead to higher achievement. Two, it relieves the teacher of planning and assessing for as many as seven different curriculums daily.

Students naturally find interdisciplinary learning engaging. When children are allowed to explore a topic completely, confidence in their own abilities increases. As their confidence increases, so does their achievement. A comprehensive report, *The Logic of Interdisciplinary Studies*, conducted an extensive ERIC search, initially examining over 150 documents, and concluded that students benefit in the following ways from an interdisciplinary approach towards learning:

- an increase in understanding, retention, and application of general knowledge
- an increase in the ability to make decisions, think critically and creatively, and synthesize knowledge beyond the disciplines
- the increased ability to identify, assess and transfer significant information needed for solving novel problems
- the promotion of cooperative learning, a better attitude towards self as a learner and as a meaningful member of a community
- increased motivation

(Mathison & Freeman, 1997)

STEM integration across subjects can provide rich opportunities for students to achieve the standards in English language arts and mathematics. Learners are directly involved and committed in the discovery of their own learning. Through collaboration and cooperation students engage in multisensory experiences that are authentic, relevant, and challenging. During science for example, my students often sing songs, read books, create art, or write to demonstrate their understanding. Interdisciplinary STEM-focused instruction allows for standards from several disciplines to be mastered in a single learning experience. One of the benefits of the Next Generation Science Standards is that this step has already been completed for you. Each *"performance expectation"* is connected to standards from the Common Core State Standards in English language arts and mathematics, as well as crosscutting concepts. In successful elementary STEM classrooms, it is hard to tell where one subject ends and another begins. An educational report, aptly called *Prepare and Inspire*, explains:

> "Looking for ways that the teaching of reading and writing and the teaching of science can overlap and be complementary could increase the amount of classroom time devoted to each of the subjects, empowering students to access STEM subjects through multiple entry points."
> (PCAST, 2010)

As educators, this is exactly what we should be planning for. Students' learning mirrors the real world. People do not have segregated parts of their day where just one skill is used. We instead use what we know and integrate our understanding to solve complex issues. The ability to effortlessly apply knowledge has been discussed repeatedly in the past few years by business and educational leaders. Because STEM knowledge is rapidly changing, today's employers do not need workers who have vast stores of academic knowledge. Instead they are looking for individuals who are effective communicators, critical thinkers, and team players. Interdisciplinary STEM instruction can prepare students to lead the future.

As an elementary educator, one of the most appreciated benefits of using an interdisciplinary approach towards learning is that it makes my job easier. By integrating subjects, elementary classroom teachers are relieved of excess planning, preparation, and stress. Instead of preparing for up to seven disconnected, unrelated curriculums (reading, writing, math, science, grammar, spelling, social studies) each day, teachers teach one topic completely and deeply. In fact, interdisciplinary instruction addresses one of the most common criticism of U.S. schools that we tend to teach "a mile wide and an inch deep," as opposed to more successful countries which teach "an inch wide and a mile deep."

(Mathison & Freeman, 1997) Integrated instruction naturally pulls in multiple disciplines to teach topics thoroughly. Studies conducted by the National Research Council support the importance of ensuring that curricula are not so overcrowded with topics as to drive out conceptual thinking. (NRC, 2007) The research also suggests that trying to cover too many topics in a curriculum with too little in-depth study can impair conceptual knowledge. Covering fewer topics in greater depth leads to greater achievement. (NRC, 2011)

Interdisciplinary STEM education provides teachers with an instructional design structure that effectively meets the unique needs of each year's class. Integrated lessons are cognitively challenging and expect students to link understandings across disciplines as well as connect learning to their own experiences. The 2007 National Research Council publication *Taking Science to School: Learning and Teaching Science in Grades K-8* recommends changing existing curriculums: "To create a successful science classroom, teachers need to modify and adapt curriculum materials so as to design instruction that is appropriate for a particular group of students at a particular time." (NRC, 2007)

The *Logic of Interdisciplinary Studies* further supports and reports on the benefits for teachers from using an interdisciplinary approach:

- improved and more meaningful relations with students
- more curricular flexibility and less schedule and subject fragmentation
- support from research on the human brain and the learning process
- relevance to the needs of the twenty-first century and support from national s standards

(Mathison & Freeman, 1997)

It quickly becomes apparent that interdisciplinary instruction enhances STEM-focused programs. Teachers are relieved of the tedious planning and implementation of fragmented, crowded curriculums, and students are rewarded with an enriched understanding of the concepts taught.

The following multiday lesson is an example of interdisciplinary STEM-based instruction. The focus is on coin values, coin equivalencies, and the Base 10 Numbering System. The lesson purposefully integrates math standards from two strands and English language arts standards from five strands to help students make connections. Pre and post assessments showed that my students' understanding of concepts and standards from the Alexander... multiday lesson were deeper and richer compared to students who were taught using traditional math, reading, or writing curriculums. My students finally understood money, subtraction, and the hundreds chart. They were also able to use reading and writing in authentic modalities to make connections between disciplines and to the real world.

Alexander Who Used to Be Rich Last Sunday

Grade Levels: 2nd (up to 5th with adaptions)

Overview: *I've used this book many times to teach coin values and equivalences, numeration concepts within 100, comprehension, vocabulary, writing, and presentation skills.*

Standards:
Math: 2.MD.8; 2OA.1; 2.OA.2; 2.NBT.1; 2.NBT.5; 2.NBT.6; 2NBT.8; 2.NBT.9
Language Arts: RL.2.1; RL.2.3; RL.2.7; SL.2.2; SL.2.4; W.2.5; W.2.8; L.2.1; L.2.2; L.2.3; L.2.4

Materials Needed:
- *Alexander Who Used to be Rich Last Sunday* by Judith Viorst
- tape/glue sticks, staplers, scissors
- colored pencils/crayons
- paper for posters and books

Teacher Preparation:
- penny master (5 rows of 10) 2/student
- sample poster and book
- 1 *Used to be Rich* template/student

Procedure Day 1:
Literacy: Begin by reading the book aloud, stopping at key points to discuss vocabulary, characters, and connections as warranted.

Math: Give each child 1 sheet of pennies. Ask students to count pennies, and discuss strategies for quickly determining answer. Review coin equivalencies.

Engineering: Students assemble 100 pennies in a strip. (Groups of 10 should be easily identified by tape/glue joint.)

Students determine best joint compound.

Procedure Day 2:
Interdisciplinary: Reread the book, acting out how Alexander spent his money. Record Alexander's purchases in words and numbers.

Show model posters. Explain procedures and expectations.

Procedure Day 3:
Interdisciplinary: Students create posters, illustrating Alexander's purchases.

Each pair presents poster. Class assesses posters on accuracy and aesthetics.

Procedure Day 4:
Interdisciplinary: Read to the class the sample *Used to be Rich* book.

Explain that they will be creating their own *Used to be Rich* books.

Explain the procedures and expectations. Model as necessary.

Procedure Day 5:
Interdisciplinary: Students read books to peers, other classes, or parents.

Assessment/Evaluation:
- Can students count by groups of 10?
- Can students identify value of coins?
- Can students explain math involved in the design of posters and books?
- Do students use correct spelling, grammar, and punctuation?
- Do books and presentations show mastery of standards?

Adaptations:
- Pennies, sample poster and book provides ELL students with models
- Make a Power Point of a *Used to be* Rich book, slide show or eBook.
- Use penny strips for a *Math Carnival* – math games set up in carnival format.
- Read the other books in the *Alexander* series by Judith Viorst.

Accompanying templates found at STEM is Elementary website.

The following sample lessons purposefully integrate science and literacy to provide students with the opportunities for connected, relevant learning experiences.

Mystery Objects

Grade Levels: 3rd (any grade with adaptions)

Overview: *This lesson helps students with understanding property versus opinion, and using observations to make inferences.*

Standards:
STEM: K-2-ETS1-1, K-2-ETS1-2, 2-PS1-1, P-SS1-4
Language Arts: W.3.1; W.3.2; SL.3.1; W. 3.3; SL.3.4; RL.3.1; RL.3.5

Materials Needed:
- various unusual objects
- story format template
- *Something Big Has Been Here* by Jack Prelutsky

Teacher Preparation:
- locate objects, poem

Procedure:
Science:
The following question can guide the lesson.

Question: Will you be able to figure out what the object is used for?

Hypothesis:

Data: List observations, wonderings, opinions, commonalities... that helps to answer the original question.

Conclusion: Students answer the original question, using observations and prior experiences to support conclusions.

English/Language Arts: Have students read the poem *Something Big Has Been Here* by Jack Prelutsky to themselves.

Ask for volunteers to read the poem aloud.

Students share observations, wonderings, or opinions about the poem, supporting answers with evidence.

Students draw pictures of either the "thing" that made the footprint or the footprint itself.

Using the story structure template, students write a story using the poem for the "launch."

Students share stories and illustrations.

Closure: Students compare and contrast the skills used in the experiment and the footprint poem. Students assess their own learning.

Assessment/Evaluation:
- Can students record accurate observations?
- Can students construct reasonable explanations based on evidence collected?
- Does student work show mastery of standards?

Adaptations/Extensions:
- Students create unique mystery objects.
- Students write advertisements or commercials for one of the mystery objects.
- Students discover ways to change the objects to make them more efficient.
- Launches *"Big Foot"* math activity on ratios.

[   ]

Once upon a time, _____

_____

Everyday, _____

_____

Until one day, _____

_____

And because of this, _____

_____

And because of this, _____

_____

Until finally, _____

_____

And ever since that day, _____

_____

The Water Cycle

Grade Levels: 2nd or 3rd

Overview: *This multiday unit teaches students the parts of the water cycle.*

Standards:
STEM: 3-ESS-1; 3-ESS2-2
Language Arts: RI.2.7; RI.2.9; RL.2.4; RL.2.7; L.2.4; SL.2.1; SL.2.5; W.2.2; W.2.6

Materials Needed:
Days 1-2:
- Free Scholastic video, vocabulary and quiz: Study Jams – the Water Cycle.
- typical diagram of water cycle
- different version of water cycle:
  http://ga.water.usgs.gov/edu/watercyclematsmallpage.html

Day 3:
- *The Rain* by Rigby or other poem
- *The Water Cycle* by Helen Moore
- ice cubes
- boiling water
- quart jar/group
- tart tin/group
- insulation cloth/group

Teacher Preparation:
Days 1-2:
- Test websites
- Prepare copies of water cycle diagrams
- Develop comprehension questions

Day 3:
- Pour boiling water into a quart jar; place a tart tin of ice cubes on top of quart jar; c over with insulation
- Develop concluding questions

Procedure Day 1-2:

Literacy: Have students glue the traditional water cycle diagram into their *Everything Notebooks*. Discuss key vocabulary:
- precipitation collection runoff
- evaporation condensation

Watch video. Review online vocabulary section. Take quiz as a class.

Pass out a 2nd version of water cycle diagram. Discuss the parts of the diagram. Read sidebars. Act out what's happening to the H_2O drops in each phase of the cycle.

Have students answer comprehension questions from the video, diagrams and text.

Science: Set up an evaporation cup – colored water in cup with line drawn to show water level. Check daily until evaporated.

Procedure Day 3:

Interdisciplinary: Review phases of the water cycle. Check evaporation cup.

The following could guide the investigation:

Question: Will you be able to identify and explain each phase of the water cycle?

While waiting for the water to cycle, read the following poems:

The Rain
by Helen Moore

Pitter-patter, raindrops,
Falling from the sky;
Here is my umbrella
To keep me safe and dry!

When the rain is over,
And the sun begins to glow,
Little flowers start to bud,
And **grow** and **grow** and **grow**!

The Water Cycle
by Helen Moore

When I was young I used to think
that water came from the kitchen sink.
But now I'm older, and I know,
that water comes from rain and snow.
It stays there, waiting in the sky,
in clouds above the world so high.
And when it falls, it flows along,
and splashes out a watery song.
As each raindrop is joined by more
and rushes to the ocean shore,
or to a lake, a brook, a stream,
from which it rises, just like steam.
But while it's down here,
what do you think?
Some *does* go down the kitchen sink.

Data: labeled diagram of experiment

Lift off the insulating cloth, and check the bottom of the tin for "rain." Have students record data.

Conclusion: Use similar questions to check for understanding:
- What did the ice represent? What was its purpose?
- What did the water in the jar represent? What was its purpose?
- How was the sun represented? What was its purpose?
- Did you see "rain?" Explain your answer.
- What else did you notice?

Have students explain the reasons for different types of precipitation in preparation for next science investigation – snow crystals!

Assessment/Evaluation:
- Can students explain each phase of the water cycle and its significance?
- Can students write in complete sentences using correct spelling, grammar, and punctuation?
- Does the students' work show mastery of standards?

Adaptations and Extensions:
- Have students make water cycle diagram on Pixie, Word or Doodle Buddies.
- Have students write and direct a play on the water cycle.
- Have students write a reader's theater on the water cycle to share with other classes.
- While waiting for it to rain, make and decorate rain hats. (really newspaper hats)

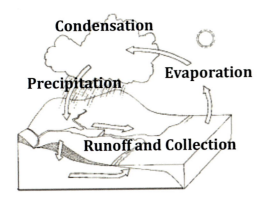

traditional water cycle diagram

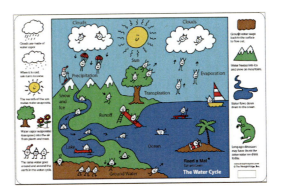

http://ga.water.usgs.gov/edu/watercyclematsmallpage.html

These are the diagrams I use to teach the lesson.

Chapter 5

Characteristics of Elementary STEM Classrooms

*STEM education relies on our ability to motivate and inspire students.
This involves creating exciting opportunities for all students.*

President's Council of Advisors on Science and Technology, 2010

How we meet the challenges of the ever-changing global economy could very well lie within our elementary classrooms. Successful elementary instruction "capitalizes on students' early interest and experiences, identifies and builds on what they know, and provides them with experiences to engage them in practices of science and sustain their interest." (NRC, 2011) When children are immersed in the study of STEM, they are learning much more than just science, technology, engineering, and mathematics. They are really learning writing, reading, speaking, listening, critical thinking, and community building. These disciplines and much more are necessary for any STEM experience. Successful elementary STEM classrooms are student-centered, provide a variety of learning opportunities, and encourage active learning to meet the unique needs of every student. The Bayer Corporation recently revealed their findings from 15 years of Bayer Facts of Science Education surveys. The polls asked scientists, teachers, students, business leaders, and the general public their feelings towards science and technology, science education, science literacy, and STEM. The analysis revealed 15 universal beliefs held by all participants. Although each is powerful, I believe that the one that particularly impacts elementary classrooms is:

> "A hands-on, minds-on approach to science education is the best way for students to learn science and build crucial science literacy skills, such as critical thinking, problem solving and the ability to work in groups."
>
> (Bayer, 2012)

In other words, there is no better base, for any curriculum, in any discipline, than interdisciplinary science, technology, engineering, and mathematics.

A child's sense of wonder is nothing short of amazing. They want answers to everything. Elementary STEM programs capture this enthusiasm to maximize achievement. Constructivism theories are used in designing and delivering effective STEM instruction. Teachers understand that students construct knowledge through interactive mental processes. Therefore, the elementary STEM learning environment is child-centered, hands-on, and active. I currently teach at a public elementary school with a significant English Language Learner population, and a high free and reduced lunch eligibility rate. The majority of my students speak Spanish or Somali as their first language. Although a growing body of research indicates these underrepresented students are at a significant disadvantage in becoming STEM literate, my students thrive. Successful elementary STEM classrooms are engaging.

Elementary STEM classrooms should be multisensory or experiential. The ideal environment provides students with opportunities to explore concepts using all senses. They demonstrate with their hands, act out with their bodies, observe, record data, present conclusions, sing songs, and create pictorial representations of their understandings. Students learn in all modalities. Research overwhelmingly shows that children construct meaning and develop theories about the world on the basis of their own experiences. Lauren Resnick describes the process as follows: "Learners try to link new information to what they already know in order to interpret the new material in terms of established schemata." (Resnick, 1983) Educators must recognize the importance of building children's experiential base in the primary grades by providing research-based, inquiry-centered, multisensory experiences. (NRC, 2007) For example, when learning multiplication facts students might sing songs, accompanied by percussion instruments to aid memorization. During science they might create stories or games, design artwork, produce Power Points, or act out concepts with their bodies. The learning is multisensory because these experiences generate one of the most essential ingredients of learning – curiosity. STEM captures the interest that leads to achievement.

Students are active participants in elementary STEM classrooms. You might say that students are the co-directors of their educational experiences. The environment is child-centered to meet the unique needs of year's class. According to Charlie McLaughlin, Chair of the Department of Educational Studies at Rhode Island College,

> "A STEM-influenced elementary classroom should require students to participate in solving (age appropriate) problems that encourage original research. Students would design, model, and test solutions. They would analyze data and report their findings to one another, or to their peers in the school, or even to others over the Internet."
>
> (McLaughlin, 2009)

When designing a second grade physical science unit last year on balance and motion, I took into account the interests and needs of my students, looked at ways to integrate science concepts with language arts, social studies, technology, engineering, and the arts to create an interdisciplinary ten-week unit called the *Science of Toys*. Throughout the unit, students explored the concepts of balance and motion with spinning tops, balancing objects, and moving toys. Children collected data on the average students' favorite toys, and compared the results to that of parents' and staff's favorite toys. They read the true story of Philippe Petit's daring walk between the now gone Twin Towers, designed a variety of moving "toys," wrote poetry, sang songs, and assessed their own participation and understandings.

> "Adults play a central role in promoting children's curiosity and persistence by directing their attention, structuring their experiences, supporting their learning attempts, and regulating the complexity and difficulty of levels of information for them."
>
> (NRC, 2007)

Students take responsibility for their learning with the support of the teachers in the room in successful STEM programs.

An elementary STEM classroom is engaging. STEM teachers purposefully plan interdisciplinary experiences to involve students in the learning process.

> "Children are naturally curious and creative. When students realize that they can discover new things about the world and construct explanations about how the world works, discovery can become a deeply personal and lifelong passion.
>
> (PCAST, 2011)

STEM education should build on the natural tendencies of children to think carefully about complex issues, solve problems, create and fix mechanical objects, and observe or understand things that no one has observed or understood before. STEM students are constantly involved in higher level thinking activities. Although reading, writing, and math are essential parts to students' days, it may be hard to tell where one subject ends and another begins. STEM teachers integrate learning to mirror real life. For instance, I often will read my class a book or have students write during math time. Other days, students might complete science experiments during writing time or solve mathematical and engineering problems during social studies time. Elementary STEM teachers do not teach fragmented, unrelated curriculums; they teach the skills and concepts students need to master established standards. As a result of the connections that are made and the inquiries that are necessary, all students can achieve at higher levels.

Elaborate supplies and materials are unnecessary when organizing elementary STEM classrooms. Although the physical space and tools are important, it is the approach towards learning that is critical. Instruction is always, first and foremost, aligned to the standards. This is necessary to focus learning, maximize student achievement, and increase teacher effectiveness. Standards-based instruction also provides flexibility in lesson design. Teachers are not obligated to teach any particular curriculum, in any particular order, because all instruction is standards-based and interdisciplinary. This approach towards allows teachers to create lessons to meet the unique needs and interests of each year's class.

The effective organization of elementary STEM classrooms is crucial in building independence, collaboration, and innovation. Supplies and materials are readily available and are stored for easy access. Students become self-reliant, and are active participants in the learning process. Students regularly work in cooperative groups to study topics in-depth. Although they may spend days on a particular project, this is allowed and encourages, since every lesson covers numerous standards, crossing many disciplines. In order to make STEM instruction relevant to students, the purpose for learning is always presented. Teachers and students work collaboratively and share the achievement of success.

Elementary STEM classrooms are exciting places. They are rewarding for students and teachers alike. Teachers inspire learners by providing "individual, meaningful experiences that speak to students' particular interests and abilities." (PCAST, 2010) Learners benefit from engaging and rigorous education. The Organization for Economic Cooperation and Development recently published *The Nature of Learning: Using Research to Inspire Practice.* The book and accompanying teacher's guide offers elements that are critical in child-centered classrooms. A few of the key principles state, "learners are different and innovative learning environments reflect the various experiences and prior knowledge that each student brings to class." This aptly describes effective elementary STEM classrooms.

The following is the web organizer and curriculum map of a 10-week interdisciplinary unit I designed called *The Science of Toys.* All of the curricular materials are STEM-focused and standards-based. The activities and assessments require students to think deeply, apply their understandings, and communicate their findings. The unit provides opportunities for all learners to be active participants and cooperative group members.

Math: Units 3 and 4
Number and Operation in Base 10,
Geometry, Operations and Algebraic Thinking

Science: Physical Science
Balance and Motion – FOSS,
Energy, Newton's Laws of Motion

Students will collect and analyze data, draw conclusions, and communicate ideas through a variety of multisensory experiences.

The Science of Toys

November - January

Field Trips:
The Henry Ford,
History Museum,
Mill City Museum

Engineering:
Toy Construction,
Game Construction

Social Studies:
Family, Timelines,
Intergenerational Interviews

Technology:
Virtual Field Trips, Web Searches,
Drawing and Graphing Tools, Images

Literacy: Units 3 and 4
Biographies, Memoirs, Interviews,
Narratives, Literary Devices,
Historical Fiction, Informational
Writing, Presentation Skills

Arts:
Toy and Game Fair, Family Pictures
Book, Second Grade Olympics, Flags

The Science of Toys
Grades 2 and 3

> ## Are toys needed?
> ## How do toys connect us to the past, present and future?

SCIENCE
Standards:

3-PS2: Motion and Stability: Forces and Interactions	
3-PS2-1:	Plan and conduct an investigation to provide evidence of balanced and unbalanced forces on the motion of an object.
3-PS2-2:	Make observations and/or measurements of an object's motion to provide evidence that a pattern can be used to predict future motion.
3-5-ETS-1: Engineering Design	
3-5-ETS1-1:	Define a simple design problem reflecting a need or a want that includes specific criteria for success and constraints on materials, time, or cost.
3-5-ETS1-2:	Generate and compare multiple possible solutions to a problem based on how well each is likely to meet the criteria and constraints of the problem.

Concepts:
- everything is either matter or energy
- energy is the ability to do work
- work = force over a distance
- force = push or a pull
- types of forces: gravity, friction, weight...
- there are 2 types of energy: potential and kinetic
- potential = stored energy
- kinetic = moving
- energy can be changed from one form to another, but is never created or destroyed
- balance = equilibrium = net force is zero
- motion = change in position over time
- linear motion = motion in a straight line
- rotational motion = motion around a point
- center of mass/gravity = point where all mass is concentrated
- Newton's 3 Laws of Motion:

1st Law: Inertia: A body at rest will remain at rest unless acted upon by an unbalanced force. A body in motion will continue in motion, in the same speed and direction, unless acted upon by an unbalanced force.

2nd Law: F = MA: Changes in the force or the mass of an object will effect acceleration.

3rd Law: Action/Reaction: For every action, there is an

Activities:

FOSS Balance and Motion: *Balancing, Center of Mass, Rotational Motion, Linear Motion*

Balancing Stick: http://www.exploratorium.edu/snacks/balancing_stick/index.html

Assessments: Toy Design and Construction Performance Assessment, Written Assessment

	Scientific Process	Communication	Data	Conclusion
4	Student followed a scientific method, and has all of the parts or steps necessary to make the investigation replicable by others.	Students show that they understand science concepts and processes. Their thinking makes sense they include pictures, charts, or diagrams as needed.	The data collected is important to answering the question. Many trials were completed if needed. Data is presented in a clear, neat, complete format.	Conclusion answers original question. Students use data collected to support answers. Real-world connections made and questions generated.
3	Student followed a scientific method, but may be missing a small part or step. Or, a part or step of the method may be unclear.	Students show that they understand science concepts and processes, but their thinking may not make sense. Or, they left out minor details.	The data collected is important to answering the question, but may be messy or unclear. Or, not enough data was collected.	Conclusion answers original question, but answers may not be supported by data collected. Connections or questions may not have been generated.
2	Student followed certain steps, but may be missing parts or steps, or the method is unclear.	Students show that they understand most science concepts and processes, but their thinking may not make sense. Or, they left out minor details.	There is data collected, but it may be messy or unclear, or not important to answering the question. Or, not enough data was collected.	Conclusion is incomplete and does not use data collected. Connections and questions may not have been generated.
1	There is no evidence of a scientific method, steps, or parts.	Student does not show that they understand the science concepts or processes. Words, charts, diagrams are unimportant to the question.	Student did not collect data. Or, student collected very little data.	Conclusion does not answer the original question and does not use data collected. Connections and questions were not generated.

Science Assessment – Teacher Version

4	3	2	1
ALWAYS neat complete correct *Exceeds Standards*	**MOSTLY** neat complete correct *Meets Standards*	**SOMETIMES** neat complete correct *Partially Meets Standards*	**IS NOT** neat complete correct *Does Not Meet Standards*

Standard Rubric Used for Everyday Assessment

LITERACY

Standards:

Literature

Key Ideas and Details

RL.2.1. Ask and answer such questions as *who, what, where, when, why*, and *how* to demonstrate understanding of key details in a text.

RL.2.3. Describe how characters in a story respond to major events and challenges.

Craft and Structure

RL.2.5. Describe the overall structure of a story, including describing how the beginning introduces the story and the ending concludes the action.

RL.2.6. Acknowledge differences in the points of view of characters, including by speaking in a different voice for each character when reading dialogue aloud.

Integration of Knowledge and Ideas

RL.2.7. Use information gained from the illustrations and words in a print or digital text to demonstrate understanding of its characters, setting, or plot.

Foundational Skills

Phonics and Word Recognition

RF.2.3. Know and apply grade-level phonics and word analysis skills in decoding words.

Fluency

RF.2.4. Read with sufficient accuracy and fluency to support comprehension.

Informational Text

Key Ideas and Details

RI.2.1. Ask and answer such questions as *who, what, where, when, why*, and *how* to demonstrate understanding of key details in a text.

RI.2.2. Identify main topic of multi-paragraph texts and the focus of paragraphs within text.

RI.2.3. Describe the connection between a series of historical events, scientific ideas or concepts, or steps in technical procedures in a text.

Craft and Structure

RI.2.5. Know and use various text features

RI.2.6. Identify main purpose of text: what the author wants to answer, explain, describe.

Integration of Knowledge and Ideas

RI.2.7. Explain how specific images) contribute to and clarify a text.

RI.2.8. Describe how reasons support specific points the author makes in a text.

RI.2.9. Compare/contrast the most important points presented by two texts on same topic.

Language

Conventions of Standard English

L.2.1. Demonstrate conventions of English grammar and usage when writing or speaking.

L.2.2. Demonstrate command of conventions of capitalization, punctuation, spelling.

Knowledge of Language

L.2.3. Use language and its conventions when writing, speaking, reading, or listening.

Vocabulary Acquisition and Use

L.2.4. Determine or clarify the meaning of unknown and multiple-meaning words and phrases based on grade 2 reading and content, choosing flexibly from an array of strategies.

L.2.5. Demonstrate understanding of figurative language, word relationships and nuances.

L.2.6. Use words and phrases acquired through conversations, reading and being read to, and responding to texts, including using adjectives and adverbs to describe.

Speaking and Listening

Comprehension and Collaboration

SL.2.1. Participate in collaborative conversations with diverse partners about *grade 2 topics and texts* with peers and adults in small and larger groups.

SL.2.2. Recount, describe key ideas or details of text read aloud, information presented orally, or other media.

SL.2.3. Ask and answer questions about what a speaker says in order to clarify comprehension, gather additional information, or deepen understanding of a topic or issue.

Presentation of Knowledge and Ideas

SL.2.4. Tell a story or recount an experience with appropriate facts and relevant, descriptive details, speaking audibly in coherent sentences.

SL.2.5. Create audio recordings of stories or poems; add visual displays to stories or recounts of experiences when appropriate to clarify ideas, thoughts, and feelings.

SL.2.6. Produce complete sentences when appropriate to provide detail or clarification.

Writing

Text Types and Purposes

W.2.1. Write opinion pieces in which they introduce the topic or book they are writing about, state an opinion, supply reasons that support the opinion, and provide a concluding statement or section.

W.2.2. Write informative/explanatory texts in which they introduce a topic, use facts and definitions to develop points, and provide a concluding statement or section.

W.2.3. Write narratives in which they recount an event or short sequence, include details to describe actions, thoughts, feelings, use temporal words to signal event order, and provide closure.

Production and Distribution of Writing

W.2.5. With guidance and support from adults and peers, focus on a topic and strengthen writing as needed by revising and editing.

W.2.6. With guidance and support from adults, use a variety of digital tools to produce and publish writing, including in collaboration with peers.

Activities: GHGR: Units 2 and 3

Literacy Connections:

Between the Towers
Momma Where Are You From?
In My Momma's Kitchen
Mirette on the Highwire

Family Pictures = Cuadros de familia
The Marvelous Toy
The Velveteen Rabbit
Toy Story

Writing:
Where Are You From?

Family Pictures Album

Web Sites:
Newton's Laws of Motion:
http://teachertech.rice.edu/Participants/louviere/Newton/

Assessments:
Family Pictures Album

Where Are You From?

MATH

Standards:

Number and Operations in Base 10

Use place value understanding and properties of operations to add and subtract.

2.NBT.1. Understand that the three digits of a three-digit number represent amounts of hundreds, tens, and ones; e.g., 706 equals 7 hundreds, 0 tens, and 6 ones. Understand the following as special cases: 100 can be thought of as a bundle of ten tens — called a "hundred."

The numbers 100, 200, 300, 400, 500, 600, 700, 800, 900 refer to one, two, three, four, five, six, seven, eight, or nine hundreds (and 0 tens and 0 ones).

2.NBT.5. Fluently add and subtract within 100 using strategies based on place value, properties of operations, and/or the relationship between addition and subtraction.

2.NBT.8. Mentally add 10 or 100 to a given number 100–900, and mentally subtract 10 or 100 from a given number 100–900.

2.NBT.9. Explain why addition and subtraction strategies work, using place value and the properties of operations.

Geometry

Reason with shapes and their attributes.

2.G.1. Recognize and draw shapes having specified attributes, such as a given number of angles or a given number of equal faces.[1] Identify triangles, quadrilaterals, pentagons, hexagons, and cubes.

Operations and Algebraic Thinking

Represent and solve problems involving addition and subtraction.

2.OA.1. Use addition and subtraction within 100 to solve one- and two-step word problems involving situations of adding to, taking from, putting together, taking apart, and comparing, with unknowns in all positions to represent the problem.

Add and subtract within 20.

2.OA.2. Fluently add and subtract within 20 using mental strategies.

Measurement and Data

Represent and interpret data.

2.MD.10. Draw a picture graph and a bar graph (with single-unit scale) to represent a data set with up to four categories. Solve simple put-together, take-apart, and compare problems[1] using information presented in a bar graph.

Activities: Units 3 and 4

Symmetry Art and Writing Project: Students will create a symmetrical work of art and describe their artwork, math, and science connections.

Math and Literacy Connections:

The 512 Ants on Sullivan Street *One Grain of Rice*
The Greedy Triangle *Alexander Who Used to Be Rich Last Sunday*
The King's Chessboard *Cloak for a Dreamer*
Math-terpieces *Seeing Symmetry*

Assessments: Units 3 and 4, Quarter 2, Math Groups

SOCIAL STUDIES
Standards:

1. Us/World History	2. People, culture, and change in time	2. The cultures of our communities and around the world are diverse.	2.1.2.2.1	Compare and contrast cultural traits one one's own community in another part of the world.
4. Economics	1. Fundamental Concepts	2. Some aspects of people's lives change over time while others stay the same.	2.1.1.2.1	Compare and contrast technologies, transportation and building from earlier times and today.
1. Us/World History	2. People, culture, and change in time	1. People make history.	2.1.2.1.1	Identify events and people and explain why they are celebrated through a variety of national holidays in the U.S. and other countries.

Activities Overview: Through exploration of artifacts and interviews students will discover that *favorite* toys have changed little over the years.

Guiding Question: *How have toys changed in the past 100 years?*

Objectives: Students will:
- draw their favorite toy and explain why it's their favorite.
- compare their favorite toy to their classmates.
- interview relatives to discover their favorite toy.
- examine photographs for clues to favorite toys of the past and present.
- conclude that favorite toys have changed little over the years.

Key Concepts: How have toys changed in the past 100 years in the United States?

Sources: Photographs, Toys Power Point, Benson Ford: Photos
http://www.thehenryford.org/exhibits/collections/Collections/toys.asp
Henry Ford Toys Online: **http://www.thehenryford.org/exhibits/toys/**

Duration: 5-10 Days

Instructional Sequence:

Day 1:
1. Pose guiding question, record their responses on chart paper.
2. Have students draw or bring into class their favorite toy. Students share drawings or artifacts with the class, explaining their reasons for their selection.
3. List on chart paper observations: similarities, differences, themes...
4. Read: *The Marvelous Toy* by Tom Paxton, ISBN: 0688138799
    A father gives to his son a toy that his father had given to him.
5. Homework: Have students interview parents/relatives about favorite toys as a child.

Day 2:
1. Students share and discuss discoveries from interviews.
2. List students' observations of the discussion: similarities, differences, themes...
3. Compare Day 1 and Day 2, record any themes, generalizations or observations.

Day 3:
1. Do a *Photograph Pass* of collected photographs. Have students in cooperative groups look for clues and record observations: *How old is it? Do you think this is the child's favorite toy? What else can you tell from the photo?*
2. Groups present findings.
3. Record overlying conclusions/observations for Day 3.

Day 4:
1. Have students in pairs go to the *Henry Ford Toys* exhibit:
   http://www.thehenryford.org/exhibits/toys/
2. Students collect data to help answer the guiding question. Students might record observations of how toys have changed, and how they have stayed the same according to the website.
3. Extension: What would have been your favorite toy from the past? Why?
4. List students' observations of their data: similarities, differences, themes for Day 4.

Day 5:
1. In cooperative groups, students answer the guiding question, *"How have toys changed in the past 100 years?"*
2. Groups present their conclusions to the class.

Project Ideas: Toy Timelines, Toy Research, Toys iMovie, picture book, Toys of the Past Play Day Celebration, Making Toys

Field Trips:
Twin Cities Model Railroad Museum: **http://www.tcmrm.org/**

Minnesota History Museum: DIY: Makin' Monkeys: A History of Classic Toys:
http://events.mnhs.org/calendar/Results.cfm?EventID=4365&bhcp=1

Hennepin County History Museum: **http://hennepinhistory.org/objects.aspx**

Literacy Connections:
Sorting Toys
by Jennifer Marks, ISBN: 9789736867375

Science in Seconds With Toys: Over 100 Experiments
by Jean Potter, ISBN: 0471179000

Student Challenges:
Recording of ideas and observations
Navigating the Internet, funds for field trips
Virtual Field Trip to *The Henry Ford*

Assessments: Interviews, Toy and Game Fair

Chapter 6

Writing the Yearlong Scope and Sequence

A growing body of research has illuminated how children learn about STEM. These reports transcend tired debates about conceptual understanding versus factual recall versus procedural fluency. They emphasize that students learning science and mathematics need to acquire all of these capabilities, because they support each other.

President's Council of Advisors on Science and Technology, 2010

Designing interdisciplinary STEM instruction that is specific to students and staff has a number of benefits. The most important is that integrated STEM curriculums have been proven to increase student motivation and teacher effectiveness. Although the learning curve for elementary educators is at first time-consuming, it is well worth the efforts. STEM-based instruction engages learners and provides teachers with a structure for designing, delivering, and assessing, quality instruction. What many teachers find surprising is that interdisciplinary STEM programming is actually easy to implement.

The first step in planning for elementary STEM programming is the creation of individual grade level scope and sequences. The yearlong plans list the skills, goals, objectives, and standards for each phase of instruction. One of its strongest appeals to both students and teachers is that it can be easily written to meet the unique needs of learners and staff. Yet, effective scope and sequences not only guide the pace of instruction, they provide flexibility as well. For example, since my district uses the quarterly model, I plan a scope and sequence with four 10-week units. Other teachers may design three 12-week units, or six 8-week units. Although, it is tempting to plan for shorter durations of study, interdisciplinary units less than six weeks do not allow for the in-depth explorations that are critical in maximizing student achievement. Therefore, to make it easiest on yourself, plan to design the instructional sequence using your school's reporting schedule.

Science is at the foundation of STEM instruction for many reasons. Not only does it provide students and teachers with a framework for connecting subjects, science has proven to engage and prepare all students to lead the future. (Bayer, 2012) Most state science standards are broken up into four strands: *Nature of Science and Engineering; Physical Science; Earth and Space Science; and Life Science.* As there are four strands, it may make the most sense to divide the year into four 10-week, interdisciplinary units focusing on each strand. The *Nature of Science and Engineering* standards, however, are woven throughout the four 10-week units. This ensures that technology and engineering are kept as key components in all instruction. Fortunately, the Next Generation Science Standards are similarly separated, and are based upon the *K-12 Framework for Science Education.* Standard-based science programming allows opportunities for students to lead the direction of learning, and relieves teachers of planning for up to seven different curriculums daily.

STEP 1: ACCESS THE SCIENCE STANDARDS

The best place to find the science standards, in electronic formats, is at your state's Department of Education website or the Next Generation Science Standards website. I have found it easiest to begin by printing out hard copies for each grade level. This allows me the ability to study all of the science standards at one time, and learn what is expected of a particular-age student. The big picture and each individual part can be seen at the same time. It also permits you to cut apart and rearrange the order to meet the unique needs of your students and school. Since these standards will be the foundation of the entire year's curriculum, it's important to know them well.

When placing science into the yearlong framework, carefully analyze the standards. Be sure the scope and sequence includes all strands and benchmarks. Understanding how students learn science will help to scaffold the skills and concepts throughout the year. I usually use Bloom's Taxonomy as a guide for ordering science standards. This means that the first unit of the year is often structured to highlight observation, questioning, and communication, while the last 10-week unit emphasizes synthesis and evaluation.

The next step in writing the scope and sequence is to find a "hook" for each 10-week unit. The best *hooks* capture students' interests and learning styles, and consistently keep science as the base of instruction. For instance, my district's second grade science curriculum uses the FOSS (Full Option Science System) *Balance and Motion* kit. In the kit, students are expected to design, test, and form conclusions about why objects balance and spin. Reviewing the science standards, along with the available curriculums and materials, and understanding how my students learn best helped me to design a 10-week unit called the *Science of Toys*. The unit was placed in the second 10-week cycle of a second grade yearlong scope and sequence. The science standards that were used are shown in *Figure 2*.

3-PS2: Motion and Stability: Forces and Interactions	
3-PS2-1:	Plan and conduct an investigation to provide evidence of balanced and unbalanced forces on the motion of an object.
3-PS2-2:	Make observations and/or measurements of an object's motion to provide evidence that a pattern can be used to predict future motion.
3-5-ETS-1: Engineering Design	
3-5-ETS1-1:	Define a simple design problem reflecting a need or a want that includes specific criteria for success and constraints on materials, time, or cost.
3-5-ETS1-2:	Generate and compare multiple possible solutions to a problem based on how well each is likely to meet the criteria and constraints of the problem.

Figure 2

After finding the hook, connect the selected standards with any curriculums that will be used. Be sure to place the chosen science standards before other academic standards in the year's scope and sequence. This will help to ensure challenging and engaging STEM instruction. Many states have already done this step for you. For instance, Minnesota's second grade physical science standards highlight the properties of matter. Students investigate how a variety of solids and liquids act and react under varying circumstances. I am provided with a science kit entitled *Solids and Liquids*, but to integrate my students' learning, I brainstormed interconnected topics to come up with a 10-week unit called *Describe It*. Throughout the unit, my students ask questions and describe answers in all disciplines, which is exactly what scientists and engineers do on a daily basis.

As you are examining the science standards, begin collecting and organizing any and all available resources to enhance the concepts for students. This also helps to keep the instruction interdisciplinary. Resources can include current curriculums, books, people, field trips, websites, available materials, free materials, and student or teacher interests. This time consuming, yet valuable, step is well worth it. During this phase in writing *Describe It*, I purposefully linked the skill of describing across the curriculum. Besides describing matter in science, students would be describing characters in reading, describing effective governments (classrooms) in social studies, writing descriptive paragraphs and poetry, and participating in Visual Thinking Strategies in art. Everything quickly falls into place once you come up with connections between disciplines to engage students. My current 2nd Grade Scope and Sequence is divided into the following 10-week units:

> **Describe It** (Nature of Science and Physical Science)
> **Toys** (Engineering and Physical Science)
> **Weather Watch** (Earth Science)
> **Grow** (Life Science)

STEP 2: CONNECT THE STANDARDS

Once the science order and focus has been decided for the year, begin gathering the remaining academic standards. Print out hard copies for each discipline. This allows you to once again view all of the standards at the same time, match standards to one of the four 10-week units, and cut apart or reorder the standards to meet the unique needs of your students. It is easiest and makes the most sense to use the Common Core State Standards in English language arts and mathematics and the Next Generation Science Standards, but individual state or district standards can also be used.

Next place any units or curriculums you are required to teach into a 10-week unit. This step provides opportunities to expand upon concepts you are already familiar with. Current curriculums and materials can and should be used. Not only will this save money, it will also save time. New elementary curriculums are rarely needed. STEM teachers just think about current resources in a new light. As a way to help me visualize the separate 10-week units, I color code the standards. This provides a quick graphic when designing each individual unit as well.

Don't worry about placing every standard into a 10-week period. Many standards will be explored on a yearlong basis. For example, students are not going to work on the following second grade standard just once: *"Ask and answer such questions as who, what, where, when, why and how."* (CCSS, 2012) Instead, the standards will be infused into the curriculum with books, songs, field trips, poems, movement, and project-based learning to illuminate STEM for students. I usually spend a lot of time searching websites for ideas to help integrate and clarify STEM concepts for my students, because I've learned that this saves me time later. Some of the best websites and materials are found through these Internet quests. One of my students' favorite resources for structural engineering is a PBS interactive website called *Big Bridges*. They also love a Cal Tech site on snow crystals.

There are so many materials available to enrich students' learning, at times there seems to be too many. Don't be overwhelmed by the upfront work required, it is just a matter of spending the time to sift through the information to find the best resources for your students and staff. Once you are familiar with the process, you will be able to quickly sketch out a yearlong plan. I am now able to draft a grade level scope and sequence in a weekend or less. It becomes easier with each unit written. Persevere. There is no better base for any curriculum than STEM.

The following are examples of yearlong plans I have designed, along with a blank template.

The Power of One

Grade 2	**Describe It** *September-November* OBSERVE, QUESTION, COMMUNICATE	**Science of Toys** *November-January* EXPERIMENT, INFER, APPLY	**Weather** *January-March* ANALYZE, EVALUATE, SUMMARIZE	**Grow** *April-June* OBSERVE, INFER, COMMUNICATE
SCIENCE	Chemistry, Scientific Methods, Properties of Matter	Physical Science, Energy, Balance and Motion, Engineering	Meteorology, Weather, Properties of Air and Water	Biology, Entomology, Life Cycles of Plants and Insects
LITERACY	Characterization, Patterns, Story Elements, Parts of Speech, Descriptive Writing	Literary Devices, Historical Fiction, Biographies, Narrative Writing, Memoirs, Grammar	Nonfiction, Poetry, Folklore Expository Writing, Sequencing, Graphic Organizers, Presentation Skills	Research Reports, Fables, ABC Books, Dramatization, Text Structure, Science Fair Project
SOCIAL STUDIES	Community, Power of One. Current Events	Family, Intergenerational Interviews	Geography, Timelines, Weather Mapping	Environmental Science, Community Service
MATH	Algebraic Thinking, Number, Operations in Base 10	Geometry, Measurement and Data, Number	Number, Operations in Base 10, Measurement, Data	Algebraic Thinking Measurement, and Data, Number
TECHNOLOGY	iMovies, Word Processing, Slide Shows	Virtual Field Trips, Web Searches, Graphic Design,	Web Simulations, Meteorology, Technical Writing	Life Cycle Books, Power Points, Research Project
ARTS	Songs, Bells, Claves, Drums, Picasso, Poetry	Toy and Game Fair, Second Grade Olympics, Flags	Weather Celebration, Snowflake Art, Kites, Squeeze a Rainbow	Technical Drawing, Science Fair Project, Insectopedia Books
FIELD TRIPS	3M Wizards, The Works, Study Jams, Franklin Institute	Leonardo's Garage, Toy Train Museum, Henry Ford Museum	Weather Anchor, Science Museum, Study Jams	U of M Greenhouse, Audubon Park, Eloise Butler Gardens
ENGINEERING	Senses Puzzles, Bubble Wand Design	Toy Construction, Family Trees	Flags, Weather Instruments	3D Insects, Zoo, Landscape Design,

Figure 3
Second Grade Yearlong Scope and Sequence

Engineering

Grade 4	**Bubbleology** *September-November* OBSERVE, QUESTION, COMMUNICATE	**Zap!** *November-January* EXPERIMENT, INFER, APPLY	**Bridges** *January-March* ANALYZE, EVALUATE, SUMMARIZE	**Geology** *April-June* OBSERVE, INFER, COMMUNICATE
SCIENCE	Properties of Water, Density, Scientific Methods	Electricity, Magnetism, Energy	Structural Engineering, Architecture	Geology, Properties of Rocks, Minerals
LITERACY	Historical Fiction, Folklore, Poetry, Expository Writing, Sequencing, Songs, Graphic Organizers	Literary Devices, Nonfiction, Rhythms, Biographies, Narrative Writing, Memoirs, Grammar	Historical Fiction, Folklore, Poetry, Expository Writing, Sequencing, Graphic Organizers	Research Reports, Pour Quoi Tales, Dramatization, Text Structure, Science Fair
SOCIAL STUDIES	Community Power of One Current Events	Inventions Research and Timelines	Mississippi River, Minneapolis, World Bridges	Pillsbury, Northeast Minneapolis, Mapping, Landforms
MATH	Operations in Base 10 and Number, Algebraic Thinking	Operations in Base 10 and Number, Algebraic Thinking	Geometry, Fractions, Measurement and Data, Number	Number and Operations in Fractions, Algebraic Thinking
TECHNOLOGY	iMovies Graphics Tools, Word Processing, Slide Shows	*Virtual Field Trips,* Web Searches, Graphic Design, Circuit Design	Web Simulations, Online Research, Bridge Design, Technical Writing	Fraction Books, Robotics, Power Points, iMovies, Self-Selected Research Project
ARTS	Songs, Bells, Claves Drums, Picasso, Observational Drawing, Poetry	Light Up Poetry, Song Composition, Multiplication Books, Zap Celebration	Bridge Models, Poetry, Technical Drawing, Mondrian, Monet,	Northeast Models, Class Play, Visual Thinking Strategies, Big Foot/Ratios
ENGINEERING FIELD TRIPS	U of M Physics Department, The Works, Bell Museum Online	Leonardo's Garage, Water Power Park, Science Museum, Bakken Museum	Minneapolis Bridge Tour, Mississippi Riverboat Trip, Big Bridges Site: PBS	Lilydale Fossil Dig, Audubon Park, GetSTEM Speaker, Mill Ruins Park

Figure 4
Fourth Grade Yearlong Scope and Sequence

Grade	September-November OBSERVE, QUESTION, COMMUNICATE	November-January EXPERIMENT, INFER, APPLY	January-March ANALYZE, EVALUATE, SUMMARIZE	April-June OBSERVE, INFER, COMMUNICATE
SCIENCE				
LITERACY				
SOCIAL STUDIES				
MATH				
TECHNOLOGY				
ARTS				
FIELD TRIPS				
ENGINEERING				

Chapter 7

Writing the 10-Week Units

Students need exciting experiences that speak to their interests.

President's Council of Advisors on Science and Technology, 2010

The first step in designing an interdisciplinary STEM unit is to complete a preliminary search and brainstorming session. I usually begin by reviewing the already completed scope and sequence, grade level standards, and concepts that will be covered throughout the unit. I have found that the easiest way to plan units is with the use of a web graphic organizer. The concise format offers teachers, students, and families a clear picture of what is expected during the ten weeks. The overview web also provides teachers with a guide to pace and scaffold instruction. Even though most of the learning activities will be STEM-focused, standards in social studies, English language arts, and mathematics are also needed to ensure high achievement across disciplines. In most cases, I list science, math, literacy, social studies, the arts, field trips, engineering, and technology in my 10-week plan. I also make sure to place any required curriculums and materials before placing any teacher created resources. This saves time and money. What elementary educators find the most surprising about self-designed, STEM-focused instruction is that new materials are rarely needed.

Because STEM education is an approach rather than scripted instruction, there is considerable flexibility in the design of each individual unit. For example, I'm required to teach four science units a year. My district uses Full Options Science Systems – FOSS kits. Although I teach all of the required science content to my students, the kits do not drive the instruction, the standards do. This is a huge advantage, because even the best-written curriculums cannot always cover all of the standards or allow for individual learner and teacher preferences. So, teach the concepts using the curriculums and materials provided, but find additional ways to engage students as well. Some years, my class uses the index cards from one kit to design, construct, and evaluate paper structures during math. Another time, we might use the balloons to make maracas, as a connection to a book we read during literacy. It is important to remember that effective STEM programs are standards-based. The creative use of materials is totally acceptable, and purposefully planning for cross-curricular connections helps to guarantee well-rounded, interdisciplinary instruction.

Once the web is complete, begin writing the more detailed instructional guide. I always list the *"driving question"* first in all of my unit plans. The driving, or essential question, provides students with a purpose for learning and teachers a focus. Essential questions cannot be answered with simple yes or no statements, but instead require in-depth analysis and research. They also provide all learners with an entry point into the topic, and are unique to a particular class, at a particular time. Although several classrooms might be exploring life cycles, using identical standards, their purposes for learning may be totally different. For instance, a school in Minneapolis might observe the seasonal effects (phenology) on plants and animals at North Mississippi Park. Students would compare the data collected to other years' research, and make predictions on future years' park weather and life cycles. The essential question for this group of learners could be:

> **How do the seasons affect your life and environment?**

While an elementary school in East Grand Forks, Minnesota might collect data on the seasonal crest of the Red River. These students would compare the data collected to previous years', and make recommendations for future river development.

Their driving question might be:

> **What implications does the Red River's crest history have on future development in East Grand Forks?**

Both schools would be using the exact same standards, yet the assessment benchmarks would be aligned to students' interests and staff's strengths. Crafting effective essential questions takes practice, but has shown to positively impact achievement.

The next component in the instructional design process is to list the standards and concepts that will be mastered throughout the unit. The easiest place to find the standards is at your state's Department of Education website. Simply, copy and paste right from the site to the unit plan. Even PDF versions can be easily reformatted. Finding all of the science concepts listed on one site, however, is more difficult to locate. In most cases, a search of science concepts on the Internet proves unproductive. Rarely, can I find information that is accurate or in languages and formats I can use with elementary learners. But, the one and only resource that I have kept from my undergraduate days is the book *Science for the Elementary School* by Edward Victor. It lists every science concept, and should be required reading for elementary teachers. What makes it so valuable is that each science concept is comprehensively explained in straightforward terms. Although the textbook is no longer in print, it can be easily found on used book websites, such as Amazon. Regardless of the source used, it is important to understand science concepts before presenting them to students. As educators, we must make sure that children do not develop misconceptions of important science concepts due to our misinterpretations. Elementary STEM educators do not need to be science "*experts*," yet they do need to be knowledgeable. Even as a science minor, when I first taught fourth grade, I too needed to familiarize myself with the science behind magnetism and electricity. We all are lifelong learners.

Lesson overviews and individual resources are listed next in the unit plan. I usually include books, websites, field trips, projects, songs, poems, games, people, or works of art. Start with an in-depth Internet search of the science concepts to be covered. This differs from the preliminary search conducted when writing the scope and sequence, because there is now a clear focus due to the standards and concepts selected. Create a unit bookmark at the start to keep all of the possible sites in one location. Do not worry about bookmarking too many sites. You can edit the list later. What is valuable is having a list to choose from. During the search, I will enter the concept or topic in various ways to view as many sources as possible. Yet, in order to save time, I do not check every listing. I avoid "worksheet" or lower cognitive engagement sites, and instead look for reputable organizations that appear to value child-centered education. For instance if searching *"weather,"* I might add "for kids," *"interactive learning," "videos,"* or *"multimedia."* I also make sure to search Amazon Books, my school library, and the public library to locate additional sources to engage learners. Place each of the selected resources into a discipline within the 10-week unit. Rules of brainstorming apply. Everything gets written down. Ideas can be pared down or expanded in future steps. Be sure to include any hyperlinks to ensure that all necessary information to teach and assess the unit is in one spot. Admittedly, this step takes days, yet it is definitely worth your time. Some of the most powerful lessons that I have developed have been created around a resource found during this stage.

At this point it in the instructional design process it is unnecessary to create detailed lessons plans, but it is important to understand how each lesson fits within the objectives and goals of the unit. Integrated, interactive summative assessments are planned to evaluate mastery of selected standards and concepts. Although, formative assessments are not usually written into the unit plan, they are continually used to guide learning and maximize understanding.

Interdisciplinary STEM instruction takes commitment from dedicated teachers. Yet, once you become comfortable in the design and implementation process, and you see the results in student achievement and engagement, you'll never go back to the unconnected, fragmented, lackluster curriculums. To not overwhelm myself, I usually have the scope and sequence and first 10-week unit written prior to the start of year. Then as the first unit is winding down, I begin designing the second 10-week plan. When you have completed the process one time, each additional time is easier. The first unit becomes the template for future 10-week plans. Simply, copy, paste – copy paste … save.

The following interdisciplinary, 10-week unit is one my students and I love. *Describe It* is a wonderful way to start the year. It creates a sense of community through team-building experiences, and fosters an excitement for learning through engaging activities. When looking at the big picture, interdisciplinary STEM captures the interest that leads to achievement.

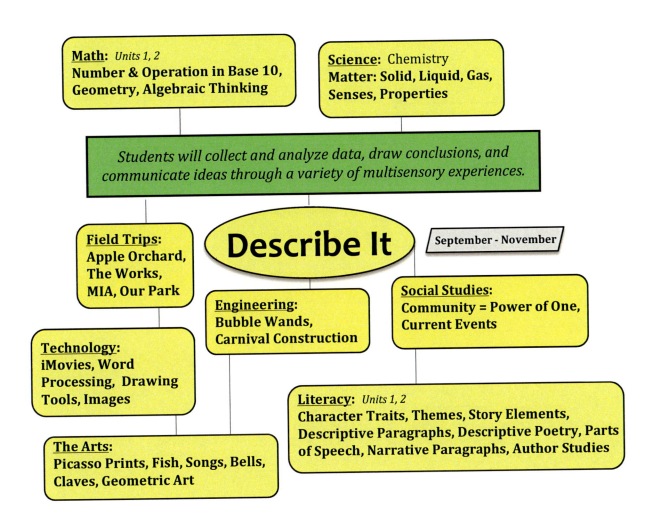

Describe It!
Grade 2
September – November

> **If you had to give up one of your senses, which sense would it be? How would the loss of this sense affect your experiences?**

SCIENCE:
Standards:

K-2-ETS1: Engineering Design	
K-2-ETS1-1:	Ask questions, make observations, and gather information about a situation people want to change to define a simple problem that can be solved though the development of a new or improved object or tool.
K-2-ETS1-2:	Develop a simple sketch, drawing, or physical model to illustrate how the shape of an object helps it function as needed to solve a given problem.
K-2-ETS1-3:	Analyze data from tests of two objects to solve the same problem to compare the strengths and weaknesses of how each performs.
2-PS1: Matter and Interactions	
2-PS1-1:	Plan and conduct an investigation to describe and classify different kinds of materials by their observable properties.
2-PS1-2:	Analyze data obtained from testing different materials to determine which materials have the properties that are best suited for an intended purpose.
2-PS1-3:	Make observations to conduct an evidence-based account of how an object made of a small set of pieces can be disassembled and made into a new object.
2-PS1-4:	Construct an argument with evidence that some changes caused by heating or cooling can be reversed and some cannot.

Concepts:
- Science is asking questions and finding answers.
- Anyone can be a scientist.
- Properties are observations that can be measured – fact.
- Properties use common characteristics/attributes.
- Opinions are observations that use value or judgment.
- Observations are made using all of the senses.
- Matter is anything that has mass and takes up space.
    - Solid: doesn't change shape, molecules very close together
    - Liquid: takes on shape of the container, wet, molecules not as close
    - Gas: takes on shape of the container, bubbles in liquid, molecules far apart

Activities:

<u>What is Science? Who is a Scientist?</u> *In cooperative groups students will define science and scientist, and present findings using evidence to support answers.*

<u>Property Hunt</u>: *In cooperative groups students will collect artifacts for a property, identify other groups' collections and explain sense used in determining answer.*

<u>Matter Sort:</u> *Students will sort a variety of substances into solid, liquid or gas.*

Experiments: *Inquiry-Based*

Sight: *Hocus, Focus*	**Touch:** *Shaving Cream*	**Taste:** *Jello/Lemonade*
Chemical Reactions	*Oobleck*	*Ice Cream*
Footprints	*Mystery Bags*	
BTB	*Slime*	
Snow	**Hear:** *Black Boxes*	**Smell:** *Mystery Smells*
	Sound Bingo	

Literacy and Science Connections: Bubble, Bubble, Matter Chatter Rap

Technology Tie-Ins: 5 Senses Bubbles Poem, Matter Chatter iMovie

Assessments: Gum Performance Assessment, Written Assessment

	Scientific Process	Communication	Data	Conclusion
4	Student followed a scientific method, and has all of the parts or steps necessary to make the investigation replicable by others.	Students show that they understand science concepts and processes. Their thinking makes sense they include pictures, charts, or diagrams as needed.	The data collected is important to answering the question. Many trials were completed if needed. Data is presented in a clear, neat, complete format.	Conclusion answers original question. Students use data collected to support answers. Real-world connections made and questions generated.
3	Student followed a scientific method, but may be missing a small part or step. Or, a part or step of the method may be unclear.	Students show that they understand science concepts and processes, but their thinking may not make sense. Or, they left out minor details.	The data collected is important to answering the question, but may be messy or unclear. Or, not enough data was collected.	Conclusion answers original question, but answers may not be supported by data collected. Connections or questions may not have been generated.
2	Student followed certain steps, but may be missing parts or steps, or the method is unclear.	Students show that they understand most science concepts and processes, but their thinking may not make sense. Or, they left out minor details.	There is data collected, but it may be messy or unclear, or not important to answering the question. Or, not enough data was collected.	Conclusion is incomplete and does not use data collected. Connections and questions may not have been generated.
1	There is no evidence of a scientific method, steps, or parts.	Student does not show that they understand the science concepts or processes. Words, charts, diagrams are unimportant to the question.	Student did not collect data, Or, student collected very little data.	Conclusion does not answer the original question and does not use data collected. Connections and questions were not generated.

MATH: *Units 1 and 2*
Standards:

Algebraic Thinking

Represent and solve problems involving addition and subtraction.

2.OA.1. Use addition and subtraction within 100 to solve one- and two-step word problems involving situations of adding to, taking from, putting together, taking apart, and comparing, with unknowns in all positions.

2.OA.2. Fluently add and subtract within 20 using mental strategies. By end of Grade 2, know from memory all sums of two one-digit numbers.

Number and Operations in Base 10

Understand place value.

2.NBT.1. Understand that the three digits of a three-digit number represent amounts of hundreds, tens, and ones.

Use place value understanding and properties of operations to add and subtract.

2.NBT.5. Fluently add and subtract within 100 using strategies based on place value, properties of operations, and/or the relationship between addition and subtraction.

Geometry

Reason with shapes and their attributes.

2.G.1. Recognize and draw shapes having specified attributes, such as a given number of angles or a given number of equal faces.1 Identify triangles, quadrilaterals, pentagons, hexagons, and cubes.

2.G.2. Partition a rectangle into rows and columns of same-size squares and count to find the total number of them.

2.G.3. Partition circles and rectangles into two, three, or four equal shares, describe the shares using the words halves, thirds, half of, a third of, and describe the whole as two halves, three thirds, four fourths.

Literature Tie-Ins:

Two of Everything (K)
Ten for Me (L)
What's New at the Zoo? (M)

Money Poem
Counting on Frank (M)
What's the Difference? (Q)

Technology Tie-Ins: Polygon Hat Fashion Show iMovie, Money Poem iMovie; Word Processing: Properties of Polygons Paragraph

Arts: Symmetry Art, Pattern Blocks, Polygon Art, Magic Pot Book

Assessments: End of Units Tests, Formative Assessments

4	3	2	1
ALWAYS neat complete correct *Exceeds Standards*	**MOSTLY** neat complete correct *Meets Standards*	**SOMETIMES** neat complete correct *Partially Meets Standards*	**IS NOT** neat complete correct *Does Not Meet Standards*

Standard Rubric Used for Everyday Assessment

LITERACY: Units 1 and 2 or CCSS
Standards:

Literature
Key Ideas and Details
RL.2.3. Describe how characters in a story respond to major events and challenges.
Craft and Structure
RL.2.4. Describe how words and phrases (e.g., regular beats, alliteration, rhymes, repeated lines) supply rhythm and meaning in a story, poem, or song.
RL.2.5. Describe the overall structure of a story, including describing how the beginning introduces the story and the ending concludes the action.
RL.2.6. Acknowledge differences in the points of view of characters, including by speaking in a different voice for each character when reading dialogue aloud.
Integration of Knowledge and Ideas
RL.2.7. Use information gained from the illustrations and words in a print or digital text to demonstrate understanding of its characters, setting, or plot.

Speaking and Listening
Comprehension and Collaboration
SL.2.1. Participate in collaborative conversations with diverse partners about grade 2 topics and texts with peers and adults in small and larger groups.
SL.2.2. Recount or describe key ideas or details from a text read aloud or information presented orally or through other media.
SL.2.3. Ask and answer questions about what a speaker says in order to clarify comprehension, gather additional information, or deepen understanding of a topic or issue.
Presentation of Knowledge and Ideas
SL.2.5. Create audio recordings of stories or poems; add other visual displays to stories or recounts of experiences when appropriate to clarify ideas, thoughts, and feelings.

Writing
Text Types and Purposes
W.2.1. Write opinion pieces in which they introduce the topic they are writing about, state opinions, supply reasons to support opinions, use linking words to connect opinion and reasons, and provide a concluding statement or section.
W.2.2. Write informative/explanatory texts to introduce a topic, use facts and definitions to develop points, and provide a concluding statement or section.
W.2.3. Write narratives that recount an event include details to describe actions, thoughts, and feelings, use temporal words to signal event order, and provide a sense of closure.
W.2.5. With support from others, focus on a topic, improve writing by revising and editing.
W.2.6. With guidance and support from adults, use a variety of digital tools to produce and publish writing, including in collaboration with peers.

Language
Knowledge of Language
L.2.3. Use language and conventions when writing, speaking, reading, or listening.
L.2.5. Demonstrate understanding of figurative language, word relationships and nuances.
L.2.6. Use words and phrases acquired through conversations, reading and being read to, and responding to texts, including using adjectives and adverbs to describe.

Activities:
Language: Pizza Pat (E) – great use of adjectives, predictable text
Poetry: Nathaniel's Rap, Fish Family iMovie, Fish iMovie, Money Poem iMovie
Writing: Descriptive Fish Paragraphs, Picasso Prints, and Poems

	Book	Theme	Character
(K)	Me First	Be Patient	pushy, impatient
(L)	Big Al	Golden Rule	shy, awkward
(L)	Chester Way	Golden Rule	creative, unique
(M)	Lily's Purple Plastic Purse	Respect, Listen	stubborn, loving
(M)	Chrysanthemum	Golden Rule	sad, happy
(M)	Hooway for Wodney Wat	Golden Rule	sad, bossy
(M)	Salt in His Shoes	Never Give Up	persistent
(P)	Babushka's Doll	Respect, Listen	sassy
(M)	Balto	Never Give Up	brave
(O)	Owl Moon	Good Things Come…	scientist
(K)	Stanley's Party	Do the Right Thing	challenger
(N)	Tiki Tiki Tembo	Listen to Your Elders	diligent
(K)	The Paper Bag Princess	Be True to Yourself	confident
(K)	Miss Nelson is Missing	Do the Right Thing	clever
(E)	Bubble, Bubble	Use Your Imagination	creative
(K)	Dear Mr. Blueberry	Use Your Imagination	thinker

Technology TieTie-Ins:
Word Processing: Picasso Portrait, Cinquain Poem, Descriptive Fish Paragraph
iMovies: Fish, Puppy, Matter Chatter

Assessments: Favorites Poster, Fish Writing, Descriptive Paragraphs, Personal Narratives

SOCIAL STUDIES:
Standards:

Government and Citizenship	3. Rules	1. Government and communities have rules for specific purposes.	2.5.3.1.1	In this country rules and laws are to be applied fairly, but rules at home or school may be different.
Government and Citizenship	4. Governmental Systems	1. The government has basic functions.	2.5.4.1.1	Explain the purpose of government and identify its different functions.
Geography	1. Concepts of Location	1. People develop mental maps of places to organize spatial information	2.3.1.1.1	Create and use sketch maps to illustrate spatial information from books read.

Activities: Morning Meeting   Power of 1 = Community   Songs
Bells and Claves   Responsive Classroom   Citizenship

Assessments: Morning Meeting, Time On-Task, Homework Completion

I've included a sampling of the first lessons from the *Describe It* theme.

What is Science?
Who is a Scientist?

Grade Levels: Kindergarten – Adult

Overview: *I always start the year with this lesson regardless of the age of the students. Besides establishing common vocabulary, it also sets the purpose for science for the year. I simply adjust for each year's class.*

Standards:
STEM: K-2 ETS1-1, 2-PS1, 2
Literacy: SL.4.4, W.4.1

Materials Needed:
- butcher block, chart, and writing paper
- markers/crayons/colored pencils

Procedure: Ask the class:
- What is science?
- What do scientists do?
- What do scientists look like?

After recording several responses, have students work in groups to write or draw answers to the questions.

Have each group present their findings with the class. Agree on the definitions for science and scientist.

My classes usually uses the following definitions:

> *Science is asking questions and finding answers. Anyone who asks questions can be a scientist.*

Teacher Preparation: assemble materials

The following questions could guide the investigation:

Question: What is science? What do scientists do? What do scientists look like?

Hypothesis:

Data: Students record reoccurring topics. As a class discuss observations and conclusions.

Conclusion: Have students answer the original question, explain and support their thinking with evidence, and any other observations.

Further Sample Questions:
Explain why this activity is science.

Explain what was easy or hard about this activity.

Describe something else you noticed or still wonder about.

Would every class come up with the same definition of science or scientist? Explain

Assessment/Evaluation:
Can students explain in their own words what science is and what scientists do?

Can students work cooperatively in the creation of the group's poster?

Do students participate in the presentation of the group's findings?

Does the students' work (science investigation
and writing) show mastery of standards?

Adaptations:
Groups could present findings in different modalities: song, movement, poetry, computer aided, written...

For older students, have groups come up with definitions for various fields of science: zoology, entomology, archeology...
(Can be funny what the kids come up with.)

Jello/Lemonade

Grade Levels: Kindergarten – Adults

Overview: *I've done this experiment with grades 2–8. This is the best experiment ever! Everyone lets their sense of sight overpower their sense of taste. You can use lemonade with the same amazing results.*

Standards:
STEM: K-2-ETS1-1, 2-PS1-1
Literacy: SL.4.1; SL.4.3; SL.4.4, W.4.1

Materials Needed:
- lemon flavored jello or lemonade
- food coloring
- paper cups for jello tasting

Teacher Preparation:
1. Make the jello or drink mix.
2. Add food coloring to make at least four different colors.
3. Put a spoonful in sample cups for tasting.

Procedure:
Have students make prediction and explain reasoning for flavor predictions.

The following question can guide the investigation:

Question: Will you be able to identify the flavor of jello using your sense of taste?

Hypothesis:

Data:

color	predicted flavor	actual flavor
red		
green		
blue		
orange		

Conclusion: Have students answer the original question, explain why their predictions did or did not change, and any other observations or wonderings.

Reflection: *The students' predictions and actual flavor findings never change! Some students may say they all taste the same, yet they do not change their original flavor predictions.*

Further Sample Questions:
- Which sense *really* helped you to figure out the flavor of jello?
- Explain what was easy and hard about this experiment?
- How would the skills you used today help you in real life?

Assessment/Evaluation:
- Can students explain their discoveries?
- Can students write in complete sentences using correct spelling, grammar, and punctuation?
- Does student work show mastery of standards?

Adaptations:
- Have students explain the significance colors may have to a candy maker, chef, consumer…
- Have students create their own color of jello or lemonade.
- Have students make advertisements for their new color or flavor of jello.

Hocus/Focus

Grade Levels: Kindergarten – Adults

Standards:
Science: 2.1.1.2.1
Literacy: SL.4.1; SL.4.3; SL.4.4, W.4.1

Overview: *I've done this experiment with kids as young as second grade and as old as eighth grade. Basically you start with an extremely out of focus slides, and have students infer what each slide is of based upon color, shape, texture and prior experience.*

Materials Needed:
- chart paper for recording data
- slide projector
- 5-10 slides

Teacher Preparation:
- Test different focal points.

Procedure: *Start with the slide completely out of focus. Then:*

1. Have students predict what they think the slide is of.
2. Have several students come up to the screen and point out why they predicted what they did.
3. Model for students how to record data.
4. Focus the slide in a little more. Repeat steps 1-3.
5. Focus in the slide completely. Model for students how to record data.
6. Repeat for as many slides as needed

The following question could guide the investigation:

Question: Will you be able to identify what each slide is a picture of?

Hypothesis:

Data: *I use the following data chart:*

slide	prediction 1	prediction 2	actual
1			
2			
3			
4			

Kid Story: One year a student asked, "Could you make it not so blurry?"

Conclusion: Have students answer the original question, explain and support their thinking with evidence, and any other observations or wonderings.

Further Sample Questions:
- What did you use to figure out what the slides were of? *(shape, size, position, color, texture...)*
- Explain why this was easy or hard.
- How could the skill you learned today help you in real life?

Assessment/Evaluation:
- Can students explain their discoveries?
- Can students use correct spelling, grammar, and punctuation?
- Does student work show mastery of standards?

Adaptations:
- Use fewer slides for younger students.
- Have students look at paintings by Picasso and create original "Picasso" portraits.

Property Search

Grade Levels: Kindergarten – Adults

Standards:
STEM: K-2-ETS1-1, 2-PS1-1
Literacy: SL.4.1, SL.4.3, SL.4.4, W.4.1

Overview: *The purpose is to teach students the difference between properties and opinions.*

Reflection: *I'm always tempted to skip this experiment, but if I do, I know I'll have to go back to teach it.*

Procedure:
1. Show students objects that would fit several different properties.
2. Students share ideas for a common property.
3. Teacher distinguishes the difference between properties and opinions.
3. Students find items to fit a particular category: blue, smooth, clear…
4. Have students name property for each group's items. Discuss how items can fall into more than one property.

Materials Needed:
1 property slip per group

Teacher Preparation:
Assemble materials needed.

You might use the following question to guide the lesson:

Question: Will you be able to identify each group's property?

Hypothesis:

Data:

1.	4.
2.	5.
3.	6.

Conclusion: Have students answer the original question, explain why they labeled the items the way they did, and any other observations or wonderings.

Further Sample Questions:
- Explain if *beautiful* is a scientific property?
- Explain why this activity is science?
- Explain what was easy and hard about this activity?
- How could the skills you used today help you in real life?

Assessment/Evaluation:
- Can students explain their discoveries?
- Can students write in complete sentences using correct spelling, grammar, and punctuation?
- Does student work show mastery of standards?

Adaptations:
- Have students select the property to gather items for.
- Have students test other classes.
- Have students create life-sized Venn diagram of items collected.

Snow

Grade Levels: 2nd (K-8 with adaptions)

Overview: Students observe crystals and predict what will happen when water is added. This lesson is placed midway within an integrated unit on *Scientific Thinking* and *Matter*.

Standards:
Science: K-2-ETS1-1, K-2-ETS1-2, 2-PS1-1, 2-PS1-2, 2-PS1-3, 2-PS1-4
Language Arts: W.2.1; W.2.8; SL.2.1; SL2.3

Materials Needed:
- Instant Snow: Steve Spangler Science
http://www.stevespanglerscience.com/product/instant-snow
- 1 container/group
- 1 marked cup for water
- old markers

Teacher Preparation:
- order snow
- gather supplies

Procedure:
Launch the lesson by allowing students to make observations about the crystals.

Have students support observations with evidence.

The following question could guide the next portion of the investigation:

Question: What will happen when you mix the crystals with water?

Hypothesis: Have students write

Data: Have students list at least 5 observations.

Do the experiment a second time, adding color.

Question: What would happen if the water was colored?
Great way to use old markers – measure water and use a marker to stir the water.

Conclusion: Students answer the original questions, explain thinking, and any other observations or wonderings.

Further Concluding Questions:
- What happened to the water?
- Explain which sense/s were most helpful to your discoveries.
- What were you surprised about?
- Explain how this experiment demonstrated the states of matter.
- Explain something else important you noticed.

Assessment/Evaluation:
- Can students accurately record observations?
- Do students effectively participate in group discussions?
- Can students support ideas with evidence?
- Does student work show mastery of standards?

Adaptations/Extensions:
- Try growing crystals.
- Use various crystals and compare of mixture to the "snow" results.
- Make ice cream or butter and compare states of matter to "snow" crystals.
- Read *Seven Eggs* by Meredith Cooper. It's wonderful for making predictions.

The following is a structural engineering unit I designed for fourth grade:

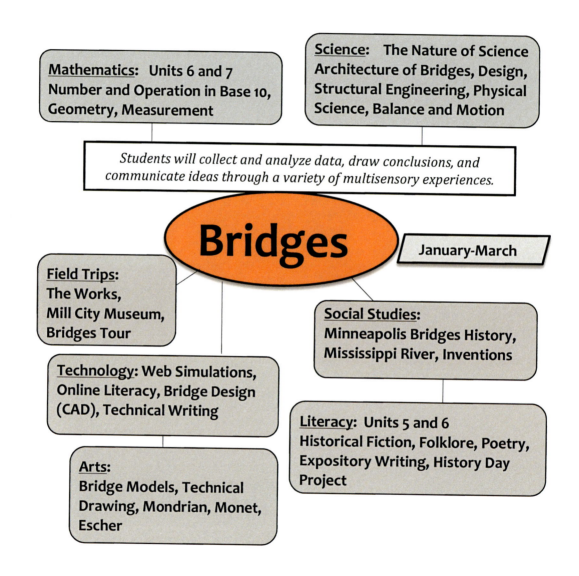

Bridges
Grades 4 - 6

What can cross a river?

Overview: *Bridges* is a 10-week interdisciplinary STEM unit designed for upper elementary-age learners. Not only does the unit center on the science of bridges, it also focuses on the concept of *"bridge"* itself. A *bridge* can span time, place, culture, or people. The possibilities for interdisciplinary instruction are endless.

SCIENCE
Standards:

	3-5-ETS1: Engineering Design
3-5-ETS1-1:	Define a simple design problem reflecting a need or a want that includes specified criteria for success and constraints on materials, time, or cost.
3-5-ETS1-2:	Generate and compare multiple possible solutions to a problem based on how well each is likely to meet the criteria and constraints of the problem.
3-5-ETS1-3:	Plan and carry out fair test in which variables are controlled and failure points are considered to identify aspects of a model or prototype that can be improved.
	5-PS2: Motion and Stability: Forces and Interactions
5-PS2-1:	Support an argument that the gravitational force exerted by Earth on objects is directed down.
	5-ESS3: Earth and Human Activity
5-ESS3-1:	Obtain and combine information about ways individual communities use science ideas to protect Earth's resources and environment.

Science Concepts: Architecture, Structural Engineering
- There are 4 basic bridge types: beam, truss, arch suspension
- load = what the structure is supporting
    - dead load = weight of the structure itself
    - live load = weight of any additional – always changing
- The load creates 2 major forces that act on a structure: compression, tension
    - compression = together = > <   tension = apart = < >
- Stable structures are in perfect balance of compression and tension – Newton's 3rd Law
- The triangle is the strongest polygon (truss): the shape spreads the forces evenly
- The arch is also a strong shape: carries the load evenly outward in both directions – everything is being pushed and pulled evenly at the same time.
- Beam bridges rarely span > 250 feet: further apart the piers, weaker the span/deck.
- Arch bridges can span up to 800 feet.
- Suspension bridges can span 2000-7000 feet.

Parts of a bridge:
    deck = surface of bridge
    supports = holds up deck
    span = distance between supports
    foundation = holds us supports
    approach = area leading up to bridge
    abutments = supports at the end of beam and arch bridges
    piers = support in the middle of beam and arch bridges
    tower = middle support in suspension bridges
    cables = strung over tower in suspension bridges
    anchors = secures cables on land in suspension bridges
    hangers = run vertically from cables to deck in suspension bridges

Science Activities:

What is a Bridge?
Define bridge: dictionary, thesaurus, other languages, own
Draw a bridge: do several times, drawing a new bridge each time

Group Brainstorm:
Students will work cooperatively in groups and present questions that would need to be answered if building a bridge.

Paper Cup Structures:
Students will work cooperatively to construct the tallest, freestanding structure made from 100 paper cups and conclude the base must be wider than the top for stable structures.

Paper Bridges:
Students will test various shapes for strength, drawing conclusions based upon data collected. (Hard Hatting in a Geo World)

Beam Bridges:
Students will work cooperatively to construct and test a variety of beam bridges, drawing conclusions based upon data collected. (Bridges Book)

Arch vs. Beam:
Students will work cooperatively to construct and test beam and arch bridges. (Bridges Book)

Truss Bridges:
Students will work cooperatively to construct and test a variety of beam truss bridges and form conclusions based upon data collected. (Bridges Book)

Construction Companies:
Students will work cooperatively to organize and operate "construction companies" to design, construct and test a scale model bridge. (Simulation)

Bridge Basics:
Students will research the science behind bridges, and draw conclusions based upon reading.
http://www.pbs.org/buildingbig/bridge/

Science Assessments:

Construction Companies:
Students will work cooperatively to design and construct sample bridges.

Bridge Challenge:
Students will design 4 bridges that satisfy the needs of the community.

	Scientific Process	Communication	Data	Conclusion
4	Student followed a scientific method, and has all of the parts or steps necessary to make the investigation replicable by others.	Students show that they understand science concepts and processes. Their thinking makes sense they include pictures, charts, or diagrams as needed.	The data collected is important to answering the question. Many trials were completed if needed. Data is presented in a clear, neat, complete format.	Conclusion answers original question. Students use data collected to support answers. Real-world connections made and questions generated.
3	Student followed a scientific method, but may be missing a small part or step. Or, a part or step of the method may be unclear.	Students show that they understand science concepts and processes, but their thinking may not make sense. Or, they left out minor details.	The data collected is important to answering the question, but may be messy or unclear. Or, not enough data was collected.	Conclusion answers original question, but answers may not be supported by data collected. Connections or questions may not have been generated.
2	Student followed certain steps, but may be missing parts or steps, or the method is unclear.	Students show that they understand most science concepts and processes, but their thinking may not make sense. Or, they left out minor details.	There is data collected, but it smay be messy or unclear, or not important to answering the question. Or, not enough data was collected.	Conclusion is incomplete and does not use data collected. Connections and questions may not have been generated.
1	There is no evidence of a scientific method, steps, or parts.	Student does not show that they understand the science concepts or processes. Words, charts, diagrams are unimportant to the question.	Student did not collect data, Or, student collected very little data.	Conclusion does not answer the original question and does not use data collected. Connections and questions were not generated.

4	3	2	1
ALWAYS	**MOSTLY**	**SOMETIMES**	**IS NOT**
neat	neat	neat	neat
complete	complete	complete	complete
correct	correct	correct	correct
Exceeds Standards	*Meets Standards*	*Partially Meets Standards*	*Does Not Meet Standards*

Rubric Used for Daily Assessments

LITERACY
Standards:

SPEAKING AND LISTENING
Comprehension and Collaboration

SL.4.1: Engage in discussions with diverse partners, building on others' ideas and expressing their own.

SL.4.2. Paraphrase portions of a text read aloud or information presented in diverse media and formats, including visually, quantitatively, and orally.

Presentation of Knowledge and Ideas

SL.4.4 Report on a topic or text, tell a story, or recount an experience in an organized manner, using appropriate facts and relevant, descriptive details to support main ideas or themes; speak clearly at an understandable pace.

SL.4.5. Add audio recordings/visual displays to enhance the development of main ideas or themes.

LITERATURE
Key Ideas and Details

RL.4.1. Refer to details and examples when explaining and when drawing inferences from the text.
RL.4.2. Determine a theme of a story, drama, or poem from details in the text; summarize the text.
RL.4.3. Describe in-depth characters, setting, event in a story, drawing on specific details in the text

Craft and Structure

RL.4.6. Compare/contrast point of view from different stories and differences between narrations.

Integration of Knowledge and Ideas

RL.4.7. Make connections between text of a story or drama and a visual or oral presentation, identifying where each version reflects specific descriptions and directions in the text.

INFORMATIONAL TEXT
Key Ideas and Details

RI.4.1. Refer to detail/examples in text when explaining or drawing inferences from the text.
RI.4.2. Determine the main idea and explain how it is supported by key details; summarize the text.
RI.4.3. Explain events, procedures, ideas, or concepts in a historical, scientific, or technical text.

Craft and Structure

RI.4.4. Determine meaning of academic, domain-specific words, phrases in a text relevant to grade.
RI.4.5. Describe the overall structure of events, ideas, concepts, or information in text.
RI.4.6. Compare/contrast firsthand, secondhand accounts of the same event.

Integration of Knowledge and Ideas

RI.4.7. Interpret information presented visually, orally, or quantitatively, and explain how the information contributes to an understanding of the text in which it appears.

WRITING
Text Types and Purposes

W.4.1. Write opinion pieces on topics or texts, supporting point of view with reasons, information.
W.4.2. Write informative/explanatory texts to examine topic and convey ideas, information clearly.
W.4.3. Write narratives to develop real or imagined experiences using technique, details, events.

Research to Build and Present Knowledge

W.4.7. Conduct research projects that build knowledge through investigation of a topic.

Activities:
Please note that any books or texts may be used to enrich and extend student learning.

Texts:

Title	Concept
Invention Book	main idea, cause and effect
African American Inventors	main idea, relevant details
Baseball's Hero With a Heart	draws conclusions
Pop's Bridge	viewpoint
A Street Through Time	text structure
Types of Bridges	classify, relevant details
The Story of the Brooklyn Bridge	sequencing
The Town That Moved	cause and effect
The Great Bridge Building Contest	characterization, nonfiction
This is the House That Jack Built	fluency, text structure
Roy Makes a Car	nonfiction, biography
Weird and Wacky Inventions	nonfiction, evaluate
Twenty-One Elephants	compare and contrast
Bridges	nonfiction, text structure
Bridges Online	relevant details, text structure
The Golden Gate Bridge	nonfiction, sequencing

Poetry
Helicopter
Mr. Mad's Machine
Bridges Poem by Glory Oljace
Bridges Rap

Assessments:

35W Bridge History: *Students will research the construction of the original 35W bridge and the new 35W bridge.* http://www.mnhs.org/library/bridge/ *(1967 footage of 35W Bridge, facts, photographs, newspaper archives)*

Types of Bridges: *Students will write a thesis essay describing and illustrating the 3 types of bridges.*

This is the Bridge That Jack Built Books: Students create *building* books describing bridge construction.

To Build A Bridge: In cooperative groups students will create the illustrated story of a Minnesota Bridge.

Bridge Celebration: As a class, students will plan and host a celebration of learning for family and peers.

MATH
Standards:

GEOMETRY

Draw and identify lines, angles, and classify shapes by properties of their lines and angles.

4.G.1. Draw points, lines, line segments, rays, angles (right, acute, obtuse), and perpendicular and parallel lines. Identify these in two-dimensional figures.

4.G.2. Classify two-dimensional figures based upon parallel, perpendicular lines, or angles of a specified size. Recognize right triangles as a category, and identify right triangles.

4.G.3. Recognize line of symmetry for 2D figures and symmetric figures, draw lines of symmetry.

MEASUREMENT AND DATA

Solve problems involving measurement and conversion from a larger unit to a smaller unit.

4.MD.1. Know relative sizes of measurement units within one system of units. Within a single system of measurement, express measurements in a larger unit in terms of a smaller unit. Record measurement equivalents in a two-column table.

4.MD.2. Use the four operations to solve word problems involving distances, intervals of time, liquid volumes, masses, and money, including problems involving simple fractions, decimals, and problems requiring expressing measurements given in a larger unit in terms of a smaller unit. Represent measurement quantities using diagrams.

4.MD.3. Apply the area and perimeter formulas for rectangles in real world or math problems.

Geometric measurement: understand concepts of angle and measure angles.

4.MD.5. Recognize angles as geometric shapes that are formed wherever two rays share a common endpoint, and understand concepts of angle measurement.

4.MD.6. Measure angles in degrees using a protractor. Sketch angles of specified measure.

NUMBER AND OPERATIONS IN BASE TEN

Generalize place value understanding for multi-digit whole numbers.

4.NBT.1 Recognize that in a multi-digit whole number, a digit in one place represents ten times what it represents in the place to its right.

4.NBT.2 Read and write multi-digit whole numbers using base-ten numerals, number names, and expanded form. Compare multi-digit numbers based on place value, using >, =, and < symbols to record the results.

4.NBT.3. Use place value understanding to round multi-digit whole numbers to any place.

Use place value understanding & properties of operations to perform multi-digit arithmetic.

4.NBT.4. Fluently add and subtract multi-digit whole numbers using the standard algorithm.

4.NBT.5. Multiply whole numbers of up to 4-digits by a 1-digit whole number, and multiply two 2-digit numbers, using strategies of place value, properties of operations. Illustrate and explain calculations with equations, rectangular arrays, and/or area models.

4.NBT.6. Find whole-number quotients and remainders up to 4-digit dividends and 1-digit divisors, using strategies based on place value, properties of operations, and/or the relationship between multiplication and division. Illustrate and explain the calculation by using equations, rectangular arrays, and/or area models.

Literacy and Math Connections:
The Greedy Triangle (N)   *Fly on the Ceiling (L)*   *Spaghetti and Meatballs for All (O)*

Activities/Assessments:
Quadrilateral Art   Pattern Block Art   Origami Polyhedrons
Newspaper Polyhedrons   Unit Tests   Data Collection & Analysis

TECHNOLOGY
Standards:

1. **Creativity and Innovation**
   Students demonstrate creative thinking, construct knowledge, and develop innovative products and processes using technology.
   - b. create original works as a means of personal or group expression.
   - c. use models and simulations to explore complex systems and issues.

2. **Communication and Collaboration:**
   Students use digital media and environments to communicate and work collaboratively. Students:
   - d. contribute to project teams to produce original works or solve problems

3. **Research and Information Fluency:**
   Students apply digital tools to gather, evaluate and use information. Students:
   - b. locate, organize, analyze, evaluate, synthesize, and ethically use information from a variety of sources and media.

4. **Critical Thinking, Problem Solving, and Decision Making**
   Students use critical thinking skills to plan and conduct research, manage products, solve problems, and make informed decisions using appropriate digital tools and resources. Students:
   - a. identify and define authentic problems and significant questions for investigation
   - c. collect and analyze data to identify solutions and make informed decisions

SOCIAL STUDIES
Standards:

Geography	4.3.1.1.1	People use geographic and geospatial technologies to acquire, process, report information within spatial contexts.	Create and interpret simple maps; incorporate map basics, points, lines, and colored areas to display information.
Geography	4.3.2.4.2	People construct regions to identify, organize, and interpret the Earth's surface, which simplifies the Earth's complexity.	Create and interpret simple maps; incorporate map basics, points, lines, and colored areas to display information.
Geography	4.3.4.10.1	The meaning, use, distribution and importance of resources change over time.	Describe how the location of resources and the distribution of people and economic activities created regions in the U.S.
History	4.4.1.2.1	Historical inquiry is a process in which multiple sources and evidence are used to draw conclusions about the past.	Use maps to compare and contrast a particular region in North America at different points in time.

Activities/Assessments:

Invention Timelines
Mississippi River Research
Minneapolis History Projects

Chapter 8

Designing Interdisciplinary STEM Lessons

One of the most powerful ways to improve K-12 education is to instill a culture of innovation throughout the system.

President's Council of Advisors on Science and Technology, 2010

It seems that every few years "new" revolutionary curriculums, terminology, or instructional models are developed in hopes of closing the gaps in student achievement. Sadly, there are no new methods or models that will solve all issues for all students. Each year's class is unique. There are, however, certain elements contained in all successful lessons: the launch, purpose of the lesson, group practice, independent practice, and closure.

When designing individual interdisciplinary, STEM-focused experiences, use the lesson plan format that best fits your teaching style and helps to guide students towards mastery of standards. For example, if I am teaching a concept for the first time or being formally observed, I complete a comprehensive lesson plan. Yet, if the lesson involves concepts or standards I have taught before, I will just review the 10-week instructional plan. If detailed plans are needed, it is best to begin by exploring the lesson's concepts and standards. Then list any cross-curricular standards to be covered, along with an overview of the activity. The overview helps the teacher, observer, and colleagues understand the rationale and order of instruction. I also include required materials, anything that needs to be prepared, and links or resources that are necessary for teaching the lesson.

As with all good teaching, effective STEM-focused lessons begin with a hook. Some instructional designers call this the anticipatory set or the launch. Regardless of the term used, this is the point you engage learners. I often start with a poem, short video, or discrepant event. It is not necessary to create elaborate introductions for every lesson, but do intentionally think about what will focus learning and engage learners best.

Once students are "hooked," the purpose of the lesson is stated in kid friendly terms. My district calls this the learning target. The purpose helps teachers and students stay on-track with the intended content to be covered. A learning target for a third grade life science lesson might be, "I can describe in pictures and words the life cycle of a wax worm." A fourth grade math objective could be, "I can create and describe the features of a symmetrical design that uses at least four different polygons." The lesson's purpose should be measurable and be based upon grade level academic standards.

The next phase in lesson design is guided and independent practice. In typical elementary classrooms the majority of instructional time is devoted to practice. Teachers and students first model the skills, strategies, concepts, and standards that are to be mastered within the lesson. I try to design multisensory experiences during this phase to engage all learners. Students then practice the skills as a class, followed by independent practice. Formative assessments are occurring continually, providing teachers with quick checks for understanding. These assessments can also prevent misconceptions from developing and ensure learning targets are met. But, what I appreciate the most is that they allow for "teachable moments." Students often make the best connections and observations when provided the opportunities to share findings through safe practice.

During the final phase, students are brought back for closure to the lesson. Many experts cite the lesson's closing as the most critical component in student achievement. Unfortunately, teachers often have difficulty fitting this in. We are so busy teaching and assessing, that we simply run out of time. Yet, effective closings are administered quickly. They can be as easy as a *"Fist of 5"* or an exit slip that gauges student understanding. Closings also provide opportunities to practice using academic language correctly. In most cases, product-based summative assessments are used to evaluate student achievement at the end of the unit. Higher-level questions are used in the closing, however, to challenge students and encourage innovative ideas. Although, I always plan for several extension questions and activities in advance, they often change based upon what happens during the learning experience. Therefore, the concluding questions are never exactly the same. Elementary STEM-focused instruction allows for variation.

Any lesson can have a STEM focus. Simply start with the standards, search for resources to illuminate concepts, engage students in meaningful experiences, enhance students' understanding with interdisciplinary connections, and allow students the time to investigate concepts deeply. Interdisciplinary, STEM instruction provides students with the experiences and skills necessary to be successful in an interdependent global society. (NRC, 2011) Research shows that lessons that follow this basic framework are more likely to involve, motivate, and inspire learners.

One of my favorite 10-week units to teach is Bubbleology – the study of bubbles. I designed this unit to teach the physical properties of matter, and how heat energy is transferred – fourth grade science standards. When planning the unit, I conducted various searches for information on bubbles and water. During one of the searches, I found a book entitled *Bubble, Bubble* by Mercer Mayer. At first glance the book appeared too easy for my fourth grade readers, but as I continued to read the book I discovered it was perfect! The book was ideal for teaching prediction, writing, inquiry-based science, and literacy. I ended up creating an integrated multiday lesson based upon this fabulous story. The book launches an investigation into the shape of bubbles. The lesson was intentionally placed at the point in the 10-week unit when students would be confident in their understanding of the various properties of water and detergents. I have included the *Bubble, Bubble* lesson as well *Beam Bridges,* to show how effortlessly STEM can be integrated into the core curriculum.

Bubble, Bubble

Grade Levels: 4th (K – 5th with adaptations)

Overview: In the book a boy meets a man selling magic bubbles and buys a bottle. When he blows into the liquid, the bubbles turn into different creatures.

The book launches a lesson that integrates literacy, science, and art.

Standards:

Science: 4.2.1.1.1; 4.2.1.2.1

Language Arts: RL.4.1; RL.4.3; SL.4.1; SL.4.2; SL.4.3; W.4.1; W.4.2; L.2.1; L.4.2; L.4.6

Materials Needed:
- *Bubble, Bubble* by Mercer Mayer
- bubble solution
- pipe cleaners, string for student, yarn…
- different shaped bubble wands
- Bubbles Slide Show (optional)

Teacher Preparation:
- prepare bubble solution the night before – Dawn dish soap makes the best bubbles.

Literacy Launch: Have students make predictions about the story from the cover illustrations and title. Discuss any key findings that come from the discussion.

Read the book, stopping at key points to discuss vocabulary and illustrations.

Have students summarize the book, supporting opinions with evidence.

Science Launch: Ask the students, "Could we make bubbles like the boy did in the book? Why or why not?"

Have a discussion about bubble shapes. Are bubbles always spherical shaped? What if you used a square bubble wand? What if you used a triangular bubble wand?

Procedure:
The following question can guide the exploration:

Question: Can bubbles be shapes other than spheres?

Hypothesis:

The data chart similar to the one below works well.

Data:

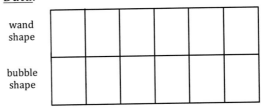

Engineering: Students construct and test a variety of bubble wands, concluding that bubbles are always spherical in shape.

Conclusion: Students answer the original question, using evidence from observations and prior experiences to support answers.

Other possible questions to ask:
- Why are bubbles always spherical shaped?
- Is there a way to extend a bubble's *"life?"*
- How are surface tension and density demonstrated in this experiment?
- Explain something else you noticed.

Assessment/Evaluation:
- Can students make predictions and inferences based on clues from the text?
- Can students explain the author's purpose?
- Can students make connections?
- Can students explain how surface tension and density effect the formation of bubbles?
- Do students use evidence to support ideas?
- Can students write using correct spelling, grammar, and punctuation?
- Do students demonstrate mastery of standards?

Adaptations:
- Students can create Power Point presentations.
- Students discuss the impact of bubble shape on bubble wand marketing.
- Have bubble wands already constructed.
- Have students make advertisements for bubble wands.

Beam Bridges

Grade Levels: 4th (up to 8th with adaptions)

Overview: *This multiday lesson teaches students the concepts involved in the construction of beam bridges, and the true story of Lemuel Chenoweth – designer of the Philippe Covered Bridge.*

Standards:
Science: 4.1.2.2.1; 4.1.2.2.2
Language Arts: RL4.1; RI4.1; RI4.3, W.4.2; W.4.7

Materials Needed:
Day 1:
- *The Great Bridge Building Contest*: Zaunders, Bo
- U.S. Map/World Map

Day 2:
- *The Great Bridge Building Contest*
- Photos of the Philippe Bridge
- tongue depressors or popsicle sticks
- hot glue guns
- bridge chart

Days 3-5:
- *The Great Bridge Building Contest*
- images and text on a U.S. covered bridge
- tongue depressors or popsicle sticks
- hot glue guns
- bridge chart
- uniform weight measure – text books, sand...

Teacher Preparation:
Days 1-2:
- locate book – makes STEM real for kids
- download images of the Philippe Bridge
- develop comprehension questions
- models of truss systems

Days 3-5:
- download images of the Zumbrota Bridge
- develop comprehension questions
- test hyperlinks and preview sites
- prepare weights
- develop concluding questions

Procedure Day 1-2:
Literacy: Read the book, *The Great Bridge Building Contest*, by Bo Zaunders.

Stop at key points to discuss inferences, reactions, and connection. After finishing, show students present day and historic images of the Philippe Bridge.

Students record observations and conclusions on a unit-long bridges chart.

Science: Show examples of successful and unsuccessful truss systems. Have students infer the characteristics of strong load bearing designs.

Students work cooperatively to design a truss bridge, with blue prints.

Procedure Day 3-5:
Interdisciplinary: Read the last few pages of the Great Bridge Building Contest which lists 18 of the covered bridges left in the U.S.

Research one of the bridges. We use the following website:
http://www.johnweeks.com/miscbridges/pages/zumbrota.html.
The site has great pictures, text and data.

Discuss the key features and history of the bridge. Look at the images, and compare to the Philippe Bridge. Students record the new bridge on a unit-long bridges chart.

Bridges! Amazing Structures to Design, Build & Test by Carol A. Johmann and Elizabeth J. Rieth pages

Review blueprints and observations from Days 1 and 2. Model use of hot glue guns. Students begin construction of bridges and record data from each day's work.

When complete, have students evaluate for strength and aesthetics.

Students summarize findings orally and in writing.

Assessment/Evaluation:
- Can students explain key features of truss systems and their significance in design?
- Can students make connections?
- Can students keep track of an investigation?
- Do students show mastery of standards?
- Do students support conclusions and opinions with evidence?

Adaptations/Extensions:
- Use CD programs to design bridges.
- Have students write a play on the life of *Lemuel Chenoweth*.

[Title box — blank]

GRADE LEVELS: _____

OVERVIEW: _____
_____
_____
_____

STANDARDS:

Science: _____

Language Arts: _____
_____

Mathematics: _____

Social Studies: _____

Arts: _____

MATERIALS NEEDED:
_____
_____
_____
_____

TEACHER PREPARATION:
_____
_____
_____
_____

RESOURCES:
_____
_____
_____
_____
_____

PROCEDURE: _____
_____
_____
_____
_____
_____
_____
_____
_____
_____
_____
_____
_____
_____
_____
_____

ASSESSMENTS:
_____
_____
_____

ADAPTATIONS, EXTENSIONS:
_____
_____
_____
_____

Chapter 9

Opportunities and Challenges

Teachers are the single most important factor in the K-12 educational system, and they are crucial to the strategy of preparing and inspiring students in STEM.

President's Council of Advisors on Science and Technology, 2010

The benefits of integrated science, technology, engineering, and mathematics instruction are well documented. The Bayer Corporation, in their analysis of 15 years of public opinion polls on science education found that all stakeholders believed that "Science literacy is critical for all Americans young and old, scientist or non-scientists." (Bayer, 2012) Not only does STEM engage all learners, it fuels our economy. Workers in STEM fields are in high demand worldwide, and on average earn 26% more than workers in other fields. (Fudge, 2013) STEM education could very well be a viable solution for closing the academic and opportunity gaps that persist in our country.

Resources for implementing STEM-focused instruction are at an all-time high. The United States' commitment to STEM-focused programming has never been stronger. Support can be seen throughout PK to post-secondary education with competitive grants to maximize student achievement and teacher effectiveness, increased funding for innovative structures, and the creation of a STEM Master Teachers Corps. The United States budgets almost $3 billion annually for the improvement of science, technology, engineering, and mathematics education. Funding for STEM initiatives in the 2014 U.S. fiscal budget is set to increase by $195 million. In response to the grumblings and questions from constituents as to the "mismanagement of STEM funds," the Obama Administration has created a 5-Year STEM Strategic Plan. The plan revamps and improves the structure for distributing STEM funds in order to impact more students and teachers. The four reorganized areas addressed are K-12 instruction, undergraduate education, graduate fellowships, and education activities that typically take place outside the classroom. (The White House, 2013) Not surprisingly, STEM instruction has also become a critical component of private funding as well. The monetary incentives to implement STEM have never been better!

Another advantage of STEM-focused programming is the opportunity for worldwide collaboration. Due to our technology-rich society, teachers can now take workshops from the comfort of their own couch, Skype with educators from across the globe, or take students on virtual field trips with world-renowned experts. The advancements due to a new focus on collaboration can be seen with the development of the Common Core State Standards in mathematics, English and language arts, and the Next Generation Science Standards. Each is a perfect example of what is possible when we work together. Yet, what I find the most exciting as a 22-year veteran classroom teacher is that STEM education, its definition, and its best practices, are still in the developmental stages. We have the opportunity to create standards-based instructional systems that attract students into STEM fields. Since, there is not one correct way to implement STEM-focused learning, collaboration is critical in designing instruction that supports student learning, maximizes achievement, and increases teacher effectiveness.

As in all successful endeavors, STEM education also faces considerable challenges. One of the main hurdles to implementing K-12 STEM programming is the knowledge of best practices on how children learn science, technology, engineering, and mathematics. Because STEM is a relatively new approach toward learning, it is not completely developed or even understood. This causes confusion amongst educators and other stakeholders as to what STEM looks like at each level. Teachers may also question whether STEM education is even possible. The use of common standards and the creation of collaborative STEM networks help to clarify these concerns. Quality professional development that prepares and supports teachers in delivering rigorous STEM throughout the year ensures sustainable and effective programming.

Another obstacle educators list is the high cost of quality implementation. This should never be the reason schools decide against STEM-focused instruction; as STEM uses an interdisciplinary approach towards learning rather than a static curriculum, it can be implemented using existing materials. Big-ticket items are unnecessary; yet, there are also a number of options available to schools seeking additional funding support. Some schools have technology plans in place to prioritize needs for when funding becomes available. Other schools develop partnerships with local and national organizations to support the purchase of technical equipment and high-cost items. These organizations can assist sites by offering speakers, mentors, internships, scholarships, or field trip opportunities. Successful STEM programs are collaborative in all aspects.

Other teachers may be concerned with the amount of time that is necessary to launch and sustain STEM. The initial planning does take a large commitment, but the first few years of any new program are challenging. Teachers who have gone through the planning, launch, and maintenance of STEM programs have no regrets. They understand that interdisciplinary STEM instruction maximizes student learning and increases teacher effectiveness. Once the STEM units are in place with an established schedule, each succeeding year becomes easier. Interdisciplinary STEM education is well worth the effort.

I have included a brief explanation of the most common STEM program models used at the elementary level.

Pull Out:

Sites new to STEM education may decide on a pull out or a push-in program. In a pull out model, students are *pulled out* of other programming to receive instruction in STEM. The pull out structure is said to be one of the least intrusive models. Since a specialist provides the STEM instruction for the entire school, regular programming is not disrupted. The pull out model is usually taught in a lab setting by a licensed STEM educator. The focus is most often on providing science, technology, and engineering experiences through project-based learning, while math instruction is usually covered during core programming. In elementary schools this may be seen as a special class in a rotation with music, art, physical education, and media. The benefits of choosing the pullout model include minimal start-up costs and less of a need for professional development experiences. The main objections to this model are the limited opportunities to study topics in-depth and the isolation of STEM. Even so, schools with few resources, wanting to offer STEM programming, may choose the pullout model.

Push-In:

The push-in STEM model is similar in many ways to the pull out program. The main difference is that the STEM specialist comes into classrooms to co-teach a lesson or unit with the regular education teacher. The team-teaching activities would most likely occur on a rotation with other grades. There are benefits and drawbacks to this structure. Advantages include minor changes to existing schedules and minimal start-up costs. Another benefit is that classroom teachers do not need to be the STEM experts. Yet, in order to be effective, staff development in co-teaching and collaboration methods are needed. This model is said to be one of the hardest to implement, due to the time necessary for team-building and instructional planning. Another drawback to the model is that STEM is often viewed as a "special" activity, as opposed to a way of learning. Opportunities for applying science, technology, engineering, and mathematics in real world and habit-forming ways are also limited with the push-in model.

Extracurricular:

In the extracurricular model, STEM instruction is delivered outside of the school day. The program may or may not be connected with a school, and are usually coordinated by community organizations. Robotic leagues, rocketry clubs, math quiz bowls, and science clubs are examples of extracurricular STEM programs. The classes are usually interactive, well researched, standards-based, and can be found in most communities. They are also usually well funded. Concerns with this model include the teaching of STEM as an isolated subject and limited opportunity for in-depth explorations. Yet, the main criticism of the extracurricular model is access. Quality STEM programming is expensive, and without scholarship funding, underrepresented students may be eliminated due to membership costs.

School-wide:

The school-wide STEM model is perhaps the most ambitious, time-consuming, and worthwhile type of STEM programming. As the name states, science, technology, engineering, and mathematics are integral elements of the entire school's focus and energy. STEM drives all curricular decisions and is a factor in every learning experience. The rewards of this model are numerous, from higher achievement for all students to the pursuit of STEM careers. Staffs of successful school-wide STEM programs are said to be enthusiastic and energetic. They are totally committed to sharing with students the power of STEM. Because of this, STEM professional development and support are necessary components of the model. However, establishing a school-wide STEM structure can be difficult to implement. For schools lacking materials, STEM curriculums, or experts, the initial costs often prove prohibitive. Also, additional preparation time for teachers in school-wide programs is needed for planning rigorous STEM instruction. The amount of professional development and collaboration that is crucial for effective school-wide STEM programs may also be seen as a drawback to this model.

Grade Specific:

The grade specific STEM program model is similar to the school-wide model. Science, technology, engineering, and mathematics are substantial components of all instruction. The main difference is that STEM programming is implemented within a particular grade level, or band of grades. Schools planning to adopt a school-wide model often begin with the grade specific program. This provides staffs with the opportunity to work out problems on a smaller scale. The benefits of the grade specific model are the same as the school-wide – higher student achievement and engagement. A disadvantage of the grade specific program is that it can lead to a school within a school, causing negative ramifications in morale and budgets. Schools with fewer resources may choose the grade specific model.

Summary: Why STEM is Elementary

Inspiration involves individual, meaningful experiences that speak to students' particular interests and abilities.

President's Council of Advisors on Science and Technology, 2010

My family traveled to Florida recently with the purpose of visiting my parents, but also with the plan of going to Cape Canaveral – the Kennedy Space Center. While touring the Cape with my family, I often felt chills going down my arms. It was nothing short of miraculous when I stopped to think of the Americans who were able to figure out how to travel to the Moon, live there and come home! Or the designing, building and traveling to of the International Space Station – wow! Unfortunately, the U.S. leaders and innovators who were responsible for these achievements no longer exist.

The United States lags far behind other countries in preparing and inspiring students to lead in STEM. (OECD, 2010) The punitive consequences of the No Child Left Behind Act have led to this loss, and to our focus on reading and mathematics to the exclusion of all other disciplines. Yet even after spending millions of dollars to boost students' reading and math scores, the United States still ranks considerably lower than other countries in reading and mathematics. What this means for our children, and to the future of our country's economy, is the importance to re-emerge as the leader in STEM fields and innovations. To help achieve this goal we must provide our students with STEM experiences beginning early in their education. Numerous studies have found that careers in STEM fields lead to a better quality of life due to the economic rewards, (26% higher wages) job stability, and technological advances. (Fudge, 2013)

STEM experiences need to begin at the elementary level to capture students' interests early. Studies have shown that scientists' intrigue with STEM subjects began long before middle school. (Maltese & Tai, 2010) It is also unlikely that students will be able to think critically about STEM subjects in middle school and beyond if they have not had the opportunity to experience STEM in the elementary grades.

Thankfully, leaders across the country recognize the urgency and responsibility in providing quality STEM programming for all students. The federal government has recommended the opening of at least 200 highly-STEM-focused high schools and 800 STEM-focused elementary and middle schools in the next decade. (PCAST, 2010) Additionally, President Obama has called for the establishment of a Master STEM Teachers Corps. This is great news for the United States, and the future success of our students.

For information on establishing elementary STEM-focused programs go to the STEM is Elementary website: http://www.elementarystem.com.

References

President's Council of Advisors on Science and Technology. (2010). Prepare and inspire: K-12 education in science, technology, engineering, and math (STEM) for America's future. Washington, D.C.: Author.

National Research Council. (2009a). Engineering in K-12 education: Understanding the status and improving the prospects. Washington, D.C.: National Academies Press.

National Research Council. (2007). Taking science to school: Learning and teaching science in grades K-8. Washington, D.C.: National Academies Press.

Common Core State Standards Initiative. (2012). Common core state standards for mathematics.

National Research Council. (2010). Preparing teachers: Building evidence for sound policy. Committee on the Study of Teacher Preparation Programs in the United States. Washington, D.C.: National Academies Press.

Cover, B., Jones, J. and Watson, A. (2011, May). Science, technology, engineering, and mathematics (stem) occupations: a visual essay. *Monthly Labor Review, 134*(5), 3-15.

OECD (2010), PISA 2009 RESULTS: What Students Know and Can Do–Students Performance in Reading, Mathematics and Science (Volume 1).

Office of the President. *Federal Science, Technology, Engineering, and Mathematics (STEM) Education 5-Year Strategic Plan.* Washington D.C.: Office of the President, 2013.

Solis, H. L. and Hall, K. U.S. Bureau of Labor Statistics, U.S. Department of Labor. (2011). *Occupational employment and wages, 2010* (Bulletin 2769).

Terrell, N. (2007, Spring). Stem occupations: High-tech economy jobs for *Occupational Outlook Quarterly, 51*(1), 26-33.

Landgon, D., McKittrick, G., Beede, D., Khan, B and Doms, M. 2011U.S. Department of Commerce, Economics and Statistics Administration. (2011). *Stem: Good jobs now and for the future* (03-11)

Atkinson, R. and Andes, S.M. (2011). *The atlantic century ii: Benchmarking eu & u.s. innovation and competitiveness.* Washington D.C.: The Information Technology and Innovation Foundation.

(Mel Schiavelli, STEM Jobs Outlook Strong, but Collaboration Needed to Fill Jobs, blog posted 03 2011, November).

L. B. Resnick, "Mathematics and Science Learning: A New Conception," *Science* (April 29, 1983): 478.

National Science Board. 2010. Science and Engineering Indicators 2010. Arlington, VA: National Science Foundation (NSB 10-01).

Larson, Lisa. "Minnesota's K-12 Academic Standards and Assessments." *House Research/Short Subjects* (2006), www.house.mn/hrd/hrd.htm (accessed August 25, 2012).

DeVol, R. and Wong, P. (2010). *Jobs for america investments and policies for economic growth and competitiveness.* Washington D.C.: The Miliken Institute.
P.L. 107-110, 115 Stat. 1425, enacted January 8, 2002.

Miaoulis, Ioannis. "Museums Key to STEM Success." *U.S. News & World Report*, December 7, 2011, STEM Education section, http://www.usnews.com (accessed May 17, 2013).

Pantic, Z. (2007). Stem sell. *New England Journal of Higher Education , XXII*(1), 25-26.

STEM Jobs Outlook Strong, but Collaboration Needed to Fill Jobs. http://www.usnews.com/blogs/stem-education/2011/11/03 (accessed January 4, 2012)

Department of Commerce. (2011, July 14). New commerce department report shows fast-growing stem jobs offer higher pay, lower unemployment. *Department of Conference.*

National Research Council. (2011). Successfulk-12 stem education: Identifying effective approaches in science, technology, engineering, and mathematics. Washington, D.C.: National Academies Press.

Jacobs, H. (1989). *Interdisciplinary curriculum: Design and implementation.* Alexandria, Virginia: Edwards Brothers, Inc.

Center on Education Policy. (2008). Instructional time in elementary schools: A closer look at changes for specific subjects. Washington, DC: Author.

McMurrer, J. (2008). Instructional time in elementary schools a closer look at changes for specific subjects. *Center on Education Policy*, 1-8.

V. Maltese and Tai, R.H. (2010). Eyeballs in the Fridge: Sources of Early Interest in Science. International Journal of Science Education 32:669–685.

Byrd-Carmichael, S. B., Martino, G., Porter-Magee, K., & Wilson, W. S. (2010). *The state of state standards - and the common core - in 2010.* Washington D.C.: Fordham Institute.

Boyd, Donald, Grossman, Pamela, Lankford, Hamilton, Loeb, Susanna and Wyckoff, James H., Teacher Preparation and Student Achievement (September 2008). NBER Working Paper Series, Vol. w14314, pp. -, 2008.

Porter, W., Riley, R., Towne, L., Hightower, A., Lloyd, S. C., Sellers, K. L., and Swanson, C. B. (2012). *Preparing for change: A national perspective on common core state standards implementation planning.* Seattle: Education First.

McLaughlin, C. (2009). Stem: It's elementary too!. *Technology and Children, 14*(1), Retrieved from http://www.iteaconnect.org

National Science Resources Center National Academy of Sciences (1997). *Science for all children: A guide to improving elementary science education in your school district.* Washington D.C.: National Academies Press.

"Frequently Asked Questions." Common Core State Standards Initiative. www.corestandards.org/ .

Bayer Corporation. "2012 Analysis and Insights from the Bayer Facts of Science Education Surveys." *STEM Education, Science Literacy and the Innovation Workforce in America.* (2012): 32.

Fairfield, Hannah. "Girls Lead in Science Exam, but Not in the United States." *The New York Times*, February 4, 2012.

Christenson, Jerome. "Ramaley cointed STEM term now used nationwide." *Winona Daily News*, November 13, 2011, Hot Topics section, WinonaDailyNews.com (accessed May 17, 2013).

National Science Foundation, National Center for Science and Engineering Statistics. 2013. *Women, Minorities, and Persons with Disabilities in Science and Engineering: 2013.* Special Report NSF 13-304. Arlington, VA. Available at http://www.nsf.gov/statistics/wmpd/.

Satell, Greg. "What is Innovation?" Innovation Excellence, April 14, 2013.

STEM Resources

Full Option Science System: FOSS is a researched-based science curriculum for grades K-8 developed at the Lawrence Hall of Science, University of California, Berkeley. This is a comprehensive science curriculum that is hands-on and inquiry-based, although STEM is not a completely integrated into the curriculum.
http://fossweb.schoolspecialty.com/

Engineering is Elementary: EiE has created a research-based, standards-driven, and classroom-tested curriculum that integrates engineering and technology concepts and skills with K – 5 elementary science topics. EiE offers over 40 interdisciplinary K-5 STEM units on a variety of topics. Not unique to site.
http://legacy.mos.org/eie/

Science and Technology Concepts Program: STC is an engineering practices centered program for grades K-10. STC is a comprehensive science curriculum that is hands-on and inquiry-based. STEM is not completely integrated into the curriculum.
http://www.carolinacurriculum.com/stc/

Learning.com: STEM Solutions: The ready-to-go curriculum provides foundational content and supplementary instructional materials to help sites build an engaging K-8 STEM program for 21st century learners. Learning.com is a completely computer-based curriculum.
http://www.learning.com/stem/

Project Lead the Way: The project-based engineering courses are designed for high schools and middle schools. The curriculum is provided free of charge to schools that register with PLTW. Classroom equipment, computer software, kits for hands-on activities, along with required teacher training are the main costs related to the program.
http://www.pltw.org/

Engineering the Future: EtF is a full-year course designed to introduce high school students to the world of technology and engineering.
http://legacy.mos.org/etf/

University of Minnesota K-12: The University of Minnesota K-12 offers lists of different programs, field trips and resources available for teachers, kids and parents.
http://www.k12.umn.edu/

PBS: The BEST website for teaching types of bridges. Photographs, games, text, and interdisciplinary!
http://www.pbs.org/buildingbig/bridge/

Minneapolis Bridges: Wonderful website with photographs, text, diagrams on Minneapolis bridges.
file:///Bridges/Bridges:Minneapolis%20Shared%20Reading/Bridges%202005%20Home.webarchive

Zumbrota Bridge: Good website with photographs and information on Minnesota's last covered bridge. Great tie-in to *The Bridge Building Contest* – a true story!
http://www.johnweeks.com/miscbridges/pages/zumbrota.html

Summer Opportunities: The BEST way to rejuvenate your teaching! These workshops are held each summer and are completely funded by the National Endowments for the Humanities (NEH). They provide you with FREE professional development and pay you a stipend of $1,200 – $3,900.
http://www.neh.gov/projects/si-school.html

Other sources for FREE summer professional development. I haven't participated in these programs, but they look intriguing.
http://teachingamericanhistory.org/institutes/
http://www.gilderlehrman.org/education/seminar_course_offerings.php
http://www.teacherscount.org/best/summergrants.shtml

More STEM Resources

http://www.pbs.org/teachers/stem/science/
Great parent/teacher website for teaching STEM to children with many more links and resources.

http://www.stemconnector.org/
The BEST site for exploring everything on STEM at the national and state levels. Sources of funding, who's doing what in each state, programs, everything!

http://www.sciencetoymaker.org/
Many ideas, videos, and tutorials for kids to explore engineering and science.

http://apps.exploratorium.edu/10cool/index.php?cmd=browse&category=11
Links and reviews for STEM sites.

http://englishplus.com/grammar/00000144.htm
Good website for group instruction or individual students – friendly letter format.

http://www.its.caltech.edu/~atomic/snowcrystals/
Wonderful website for showing snowflakes. Great companion for *Snowflake Bentley*.

http://www.theworks.org/index.html
Amazing field trip destination for Twin Cities schools. *The Works!* offers interactive exhibits and fabulous workshops for students. Funding is available!

http://www.primarygames.com/math/mathlines/index.htm
Good site for math facts practice for whole group of individual instruction.

http://www.sylvandellpublishing.com/ebooks.php
Wonderful site for acquiring children's books for interdisciplinary, STEM instruction. You can purchase eBooks or traditional books.

http://abullseyeview.com/video-target-rube-goldberg-machine/
Video of the most elaborate, inspiring *Rube Goldberg machine*. Build a lesson based on the video: predicting, inferring, data collection, graphing and evidence supported summarizing statements, conclusions. Produced by students and staff from St. Olaf College (*my son's college:*) for Target.

http://www.fi.edu/learn/
The Franklin Institute, an inspiring museum in Philadelphia, offers a wealth of opportunities and information at their site. Great for all ages.

http://teacher.scholastic.com/activities/studyjams/water_cycle/
Free Scholastic videos on science concepts, with vocabulary section and online quiz. I use the water cycle video to launch the topic of the water cycle.

http://www.corestandards.org/
Not truly a STEM site, but valuable information on the Common Core State Standards Initiative.

http://ga.water.usgs.gov/edu/watercyclematsmallpage.html
A link to the best colorful, kid friendly, diagram of the water cycle.. Great for comparing to traditional water cycle diagrams.

http://www.scholastic.com/bookwizard/
Another not strictly STEM resource, yet invaluable to teachers. Levels almost any book.

http://illuminations.nctm.org/
Wonderful activities for and online resources for students that support the Common Core State Standards in Mathematics.

www.nextgenscience.org/
Best place to download copies of the Next Generation Science Standards by grade level.

STEM Funding Resources

There are many grants available through the federal government. The website is easy to use and offers detailed information on each of the grants.
http://www.grants.gov

Secor Strategies, located right next door to the Kennedy Space Center, specializes in STEM proposal development and STEM program management.
http://stemgrants.com/

The United States Department of Education offers various opportunities for funding interdisciplinary STEM education.
http://www2.ed.gov/fund/grants-apply.html

Nspires lists NASA's research announcements and provides information on funding opportunities through NASA programming.
http://nspires.nasaprs.com/external/

The National Science Foundation offers a wide variety of funding for science-based projects.
http://www.nsf.gov/funding/

Motorola Solutions dedicates millions of dollars each year for STEM projects, professional development, and technology integration.
http://www.connecttotech.org/grants-and-funding

Grant Wrangler is a free resource for locating math education grants, technology school grants, and science grants for K-12 schools and teachers.
http://www.grantwrangler.com/STEMresources.html

Lego Education provides a comprehensive listing of federal and private funding for STEM.
http://www.legoeducation.us/eng/grants/

Google funds projects, programs and opportunities for STEM initiatives. Award amounts range from $10,000 - $25,000.
http://www.google.com/edu/rise/

Free monthly newsletter that lists funding opportunities.
http://www.schoolfundingcenter.info/

The 100Kin10 movement was developed to ensure every child has access to quality STEM education by recruiting, training, hiring, and supporting excellent STEM teachers.
http://www.100kin10.org/

The National Science Teachers Association offers many resources for STEM funding.
http://www.nsta.org/

Books for Interdisciplinary Math Instruction

Number Sense:
On Beyond a Million –Schwartz
100 Days of Cool – Murphy
Button Box – Reid, Margarette
Little Numbers and Pictures That Show Just How Little They Are – Packard, Edward
Teeth, Tails, and Tentacles: An Animal Counting Book – Wormell, Christopher
Place for Zero – Murphy
Grapes of Math – Tang
Leaping Lizards - Murphy
M&M's Counting Book – McGrath
Counting Creatures from Sky to Sea – Lesser
Warthogs in the Kitchen – Edwards
Counting on Frank – Clement, Rod
One Odd Day/ My Even Day – Fisher and Sneed

Telling Time:
Bunny Day: Telling Time from Breakfast to Bedtime – Walton, Rick
Cluck O'Clock – Gray, Kes
How Long? – Dale, Elizabeth
It's About Time! – Murphy
It's About Time, Max! – Richards, Kitty
Little Rabbits' First Time Book – Baker, Alan
Me Counting Time from Seconds to Centuries – Sweeney, Joan
Telling Time – Older, Jules
What Time Is It, Mr. Crocodile? – Sierra, Judy
Pigs on a Blanket - McGinley-Nally

Fractions:
My Half Day –Fisher, Doris and Sneed, Dani
Fraction Fun – David Adler
Piece=Part = Portion: Fractions = Decimals = Percent – Gifford
Apple Fractions – Pallotta, Jerry
Polar Bear Math: Learning about Fractions from Klondike and Snow – Nagda, Ann
Grizzly Gazette – Murphy

Area & Perimeter:
Spaghetti and Meatballs for All! – Burns

Capacity & Liquid Measurement:
Room for Ripley – Murphy
What's Your Angle, Pythagoras? – Ellis, Julie
Wing on a Flea: A Book about Shape – Emberley, Ed
Let's Fly a Kite – Murphy

Addition and Subtraction:
One Grain of Rice – Demi BEST
Ten for Me –Mariconda, Barbara
Domino Addition – Long, Lynette
Elevator Magic – Murphy
One Guinea Pig is Not Enough – Duke, Kae
Shark Swimathon – Murphy
Twenty is Too Many – Duke, Kate
Two Ways to Count to Ten – Dee

Multiplication and Division:
Anno's Series– Anno
Arctic Fives Arrive – Pinczes
Bats on Parade – Appelt
Each Orange Had 8 Slices – Giganti, Paul
One Hundred Hungry Ants – Pinczes
Divide and Ride - Murphy
Great Divide – Dodds
King's Commissioners – Friedman
Remainder of One - Pinczes
Best of Times – Tang, Greg
Double the Ducks – Murphy

Measurement and Problem-Solving:
Counting on Frank – Rod Clement
How Tall, How Short, How Faraway – Adler, David
Twelve Snails to One Lizard - Hightower
Librarian Who Measured the Earth – Lasky, Era
Anno's Hat Tricks – Anno
David Inchworm and a Half – Pinczes, Elinor
Inch by Inch – Lionni, Leo
Mighty Maddie – Murphy
Millions to Measure – Schwartz, David
Five Creatures – Jenkins, Emily
Riddle-iculous Math – Holub, Joan
Marvelous Math: a Book of Poems – Hopkins
G is for Googol – Schwartz
If Dogs Were Dinosaurs – Schwartz
Only One – Harshman
If You Hopped Like a Frog – Schwartz
Great Graph Contest - Leedy

Geometry:
Elephants on Board – MacDonald
Grandfather Tang's Story – Tompett
Greedy Triangle – Burns
Hamster Champs – Murphy
Sir Cumference Series – Neuschwander

Books for Interdisciplinary Instruction

Simile
Quick as a Cricket, Audrey Wood
Owl Moon, Jane Yolen
The Rough Faced Girl, Rafe Martin
Come on Rain, Karen Hesse
Knots on a Counting Rope, by Bill Martin
Black Cat, Christopher Myers
Snowflake Bentley, Jacqueline Martin
Quick as a Cricket, Audrey Wood
Dragonwagon, Jemima Remembers.
The Bicycle Man, Allen Say
Night Noises, Mem Fox
Chet Gecko, Bruce Hale

Metaphor
In November, Cynthia Rylant
The Girl Who Loved Horses, Paul Goble
A Turkey For Thanksgiving, Eve Bunting
Cat, What is That?, Tony Johnston
Mrs. Spitzer's Garden, Edith Pattou
The Search for Delicious, Natalie Babbitt

Alliteration
Alligators all Around, Maurice Sendak
Clara Caterpillar, Pamela Duncan Edwards
Four Famished Foxes, Pamela Duncan Edwards
Some Smug Slug, Pamela Duncan Edwards
The Worry Warts, Pamela Duncan Edwards
Animalia, Graeme Base
Alison's Zinnia, Anita Lobel
K is for a Kissing Kangaroo, Giles Andreae
A is for Annabelle, Tasja Tudor
Q is for Duck, Mary Elting and Michael Folson
Me First, Helen Lester

Hyperbole
How Much can a Bear Bare?, Brian P. Cleary
Comes a Wind, Linda White
Hog-Eye, Susan Meddaugh
Library Lil, Suzanne Williams
The Bunyans, Audrey Wood

Idioms
Parts, Tedd Arnold
More Parts, Tedd Arnold
A Little Pigeon Toad, Fred Gwyne
A Chocolate Moose, Fred Gwyne
The Sixteen-Hand Horse, Fred Gwyne
Amelia Bedelia Series, Peggy Parish

Onomatopoeia
Clara Caterpillar, Pamela Duncan
Click Clack Moo: Cows That Type,
Dorothy Cronin
Rattletrap Car, Phyllis Root and Jill Barton
Ghost's Hour, Spook's Hour, Eve Bunting
Alison's Zinnia, Anita Lobel
Bear Snores On,
Karma Wilson and Jane Chapman
Night In the Barn, Faye Gibbons;
Achoo! Bang! Crash! The Noisy Alphabet,
Ross McDonald
Stellaluna, Janell Cannon
The Umbrella, Jan Brett
Little Red Cowboy Hat, Lowell, Susan
Thunder Cake, Patrica Pollaco

Personification
Brave Irene, William Steig
Ant Bully, John Nickle
The Tub People,
Pam Conrad and Richard Egielski
Dinner at the Panda Palace,
Stephanie Calmenson
Book! Book! Book!, Deborah Bruss;
Cock-a-Moo-Moo, Dallas-Conte
Mole Music, David McPhail
Wolf!, Becky Bloom

Homophones
The King Who Rained, Fred Gwynne
The Sixteen-Hand Horse, Fred Gwyne
Amelia Bedelia Series, Peggy Parish
Bunnicula, James Howe
Which Witch is Which?, Pat Hutchins

Circular Stories
If You Give a Mouse a Cookie, Laura Numeroff
The Tiny Seed, Eric Carle
Flotsam, David Wiesner
The Napping House, Wood
50 Below Zero, Robert Munsch
Miss Birdie Chose a Shovel, Leslie Connor
Bubble Gum, Bubble Gum, Lisa Wheeler
Black and White, David Macaulay
House Is a House for Me, Mary Ann Hoberman
Fortunately, Remy Charlip
Cows Can't Fly, David Milgrim
Tuesday, David Wiesner

More Books for Interdisciplinary Instruction

Circular Stories
Chicka, Chicka, Boom, Boom, Bill Martin Jr.
The Umbrella, Jan Brett
It Wasn't My Fault, Helen Lester
Round Trip, Ann Jonas
Time to Sleep, Denise Fleming
Welcome Comfort, Patricia Polacco
My Lucky Day, Keiko Kasza
The Ox-Cart Man, Donald Hall
How to Make an Apple Pie and See the World, Majorie Priceman
No Jumping on the Bed, Tedd Arnold
Tuesday, David Wiesner
One-Dog Canoe, Mary Casanova
Big Pumpkin, Erica Silverman
Nothing Much Happened Today, Mary Blount Christian
Mr. Willowby's Christmas Tree, Robert Barry
My Friend Rabbit, Eric Rohmann
My Mama Had a Dancing Heart, Libba Moore Gray
The Gold Coin, Alma Flor Ada
When the Elephant Walks, Keiko Kasza
All In One Hour, Susan Stevens Crummel

Persuasive Writing
I Wanna Iguana, Karen Kaufman Orloff
Don't Let The Pigeon Drive the Bus, Mo Willems
My Lucky Day, Keiko Kasza
Duck for President, Doreen Cronin
Can I Keep Him?, Steven Kellogg
Earrings!, Judith Viorst
The Best Pet of All, David LaRochelle

Golden Rule
Big Al, Andrew Clements
Chestor's Way, Kevin Henkes
Chrysanthemum, Kevin Henkes
Lilly's Purple Plastic Purse, Kevin Henkes
Hooway for Wodney Rat, Helen Lester
Me First, Helen Lester
Tikki Tikki Tembo, Arlene Mosel
Babushka's Doll, Patricia Polacco
Scrambled Eggs and Spider Legs, Gary Hogg

Beginning, Middle, End
Beatrice Doesn't Want To, Laura Numeroff
Henry and Mudge, Cynthia Rylant
Froggy Gets Dressed, Jonathan London
Cook-A-Doodle-Doo, Janet Stevens
Bedtime For Frances, Russell Hoban
Ben's Trumpet, Rachel Isadora
Masai and I, Virginia Kroll
Inch by Inch, Leo Lionni
Mirette On the High Wire, Emily Arnold McCully
Tops and Bottoms, Janet Stevens

Memoirs
Song and Dance Man, Ackerman
The Two of Them, Aliki
More than Anything, Else Bradby
Butterfly House, Eve Bunting
The Lotus Seed, Sherry Garland
My Mama Had a Dancing Heart, Libba Gray
Grandpa's Face, Eloise Greenfield
My Great-Aunt Arizona, Houston
Aunt Flossie's Hats, Elizabeth Fitzgerald Howard
Virgie Goes to School with Us Boys, Elizabeth Fitzgerald Howard
All the Places to Love, Patricia MacLachlan
What You Know First, Patricia MacLachlan
The Potato Man, Megan McDonald
Molly Bannaky, Alice McGill
The Rag Coat, Lauren A. Mills
Uncle Ted's Barbershop; Betty Doll; Chicken Sunday; Meteor!; Mrs. Katz and Tush; My Ol' Man; My Rotten Redheaded Older Brother; Thunder Cake, Polacco, Patrica
Dinner at Aunt Connie's House, Faith Ringgold
The Relatives Came, Cynthia Rylant
When I Was Young in the Mountains, Rylant
Grandfather's Journey, Rylant
Owl Moon, Jane Yolen
Momma, Where are You From, Marie Bradby

> **Find more interdisciplinary STEM resources at:**
> http://www.elementarystem.com

Notes